MELBOURNE SCHOOL OF THEOLOGY

PARADOSIS

Volume No. 3

Christology

2016

PARADOSIS

No 3. (2016)

ISSN 2203-4951

ISBN 978-0-9876154-1-1

© 2017 Melbourne School of Theology. All rights reserved.

Executive Editor
Justin Tan

Principal Editor
Colin Kruse

Issue Editor
Michael Bräutigam

Assistant Editor
Ben Chenoweth

Production and Cover Design
Ho-yuin Chan

A Publication of the Melbourne School of Theology
5 Burwood Highway, Wantirna, Victoria 3152, Australia
PO Box 6257, Vermont South, Victoria 3133, Australia
Ph: +61 3 9881 7800, Fax: +61 3 9800 0121
mstpress@mst.edu.au, www.mst.edu.au

Opinions and conclusions published in PARADOSIS are those of the authors and do not necessarily represent the views of the Editors or the Melbourne School of Theology.

Principal Editor's Introduction to *PARADOSIS* 5

Editorial 7

ARTICLES

Pastoral Reflections on Union with Christ: Jesus' Personal, Relational Presence in the World Today
    Thomas Kimber 10

Who Did Jesus Think He Was? Jesus' Self-Understanding in the Synoptic Gospels
    Greg Forbes 20

Your Kingdom Come, Your Will Be Done: An Analysis of Matthew 6:10
    Andrew Mitchell 38

Facing Polemics Head On: Learning Christology "From the Side"
    Christoph Ochs 52

The Kenotic Christology of P. T. Forsyth
    Bradley M. Penner 64

'Zeig uns durch deine Passion': The Christology of Bach's St John Passion
    Andreas Loewe 79

Welcoming Strangers in the Name of Christ: Abraham Kuyper and the Ethics of Political Discipleship
    Michael Bräutigam 91

BOOK REVIEWS

Chenoweth, Ben. *The Ephesus Scroll* and *The Corinth Letters*
    Colin Kruse 103

Crysdale, Cynthia S. W., and Neil Ormerod, *Creator God, Evolving World*

    Andrew Brown 104

Mason, Karen. *Preventing Suicide: A Handbook for Pastors, Chaplains and Pastoral Counselors*

    Astrid Staley 107

Rau, Gerald. *Mapping the Origins Debate*

    Andrew Brown 108

Invitation for Papers   112

Notes for Contributors   113

PRINCIPAL EDITOR'S INTRODUCTION TO *PARADOSIS*

The Melbourne School of Theology (MST) is committed to pursuing excellence in learning, research and the highest possible standard of scholarship in theological education, an area in which we are called to make a contribution to the work of the gospel.

This journal is entitled *PARADOSIS*, a Greek word meaning 'tradition'. *PARADOSIS* is chosen as the title of the journal because it expresses the sense that the theological enterprise is a continuous ministry, the ongoing 'traditioning' responsibility of the Christian church to carry forward the deposit of faith from the past, while rearticulating it in dialogue with the contexts, mindsets and issues of current culture.

Admittedly, 'tradition' can have negative connotations, as in Jesus' criticisms of scribes and Pharisees who broke the commandments of God for the sake of their human traditions. However, it has positive connotations when used in relation to the gospel of Christ and the fundamental Christian teachings received and passed on by the apostles. These form the bedrock of the Christian faith. Early believers were urged to hold fast to, contend for, and pass on this tradition.

The theological implications of the gospel traditions occupied the best minds in Christendom during the early centuries following the apostolic age. The consensual conclusions they reached constitute Christian orthodoxy and the basis of subsequent theological endeavours down through the Middle Ages, the Reformation period, the Enlightenment, and the theological enterprise today.

Christian theology must serve pastoral ministry, evangelism, cross cultural mission and inter-faith dialogue. From the earliest centuries Christian leaders, evangelists and apologists sought to apply theology to the pastoral needs of believers and commend the faith to others. In recent times these disciplines have flourished and are producing their own traditions.

PARADOSIS will showcase articles in biblical studies and theology. A future journal planned by MST, *PRAXIS*, will provide opportunity for the publication of articles in pastoral ministry, evangelism, mission and other living faiths.

Dr Colin G. Kruse
Principal Editor

EDITORIAL

Melbourne School of Theology hosted its inaugural *PARADOSIS* conference on 15 August 2016. The conference theme was "Jesus Christ – For us today" and the speakers discussed the person and work of Jesus Christ from various angles, ranging from New Testament studies and systematic theology to historical theology and even musicology.

I am delighted to present some of the contributions in this third issue of MST's *PARADOSIS* journal.

Thomas Kimber, Senior Lecturer in Missional and Pastoral Theology at MST, kicked off the conference with some pastoral reflections on our union with Christ. In his essay, Kimber focuses on recent research on religion in America and Australia which suggests a growing belief in a God who is distant and uncaring. He counters any contemporary deistic notions by turning our attention to the person of Jesus Christ, God in flesh who came near and lived among us. With his distinct pastoral emphasis, Thomas Kimber encourages ministers of Jesus Christ to nurture their own life of intimacy with Jesus so that they can help others to experience the reality of Jesus as the healer of their soul, the healer of their relationships, the core of their identity and the purpose for their existence.

"Who Did Jesus Think He Was?" asks Greg Forbes, Department Head of Biblical Studies at MST. He puts forward the argument that Jesus operated with a demonstrable self-understanding in the Synoptic Gospels. Although rejecting popular conceptions of Messiah, Jesus saw himself as fulfilling this vocation in terms of the Suffering Servant, Forbes claims. Through a number of sayings and actions he also linked himself with divine Wisdom, and in some sense perceived himself as the embodiment of Wisdom. Whilst Jesus does not elaborate on his person in terms of a Nicene and post-Nicene Christology, Greg Forbes argues, he clearly understood himself to be the unique Son of God in a way that enabled him to share divine rule and prerogatives. In times where scholars (such as Bart Ehrman in his recent work, *How Jesus became God*, for instance) continue to raise doubts about Jesus' self-understanding, Forbes' essay is a much welcomed contribution to this debate.

Andrew Mitchell, MTh student at MST, presents a closer examination of some petitions of the Lord's Prayer (focussing in particular on Matthew 6:10, "Your kingdom come, your will be done, on earth as it is in heaven.") He makes the case that – contrary to common understanding – the second petition of the Lord's prayer is actually a prayer for the eschatological ushering in of the kingdom of God. Mitchell argues that it cannot have the sense of a gradual coming of the kingdom. The third petition, he claims, is a prayer that God's sovereign purposes come about. It is not, as is often suggested, a prayer for the increase in obedience to God's will. Mitchell's valuable contribution offers a fresh perspective with a view to our understanding of this important New Testament passage.

Christoph Ochs, lecturer at Worldview Centre for Intercultural Studies (Tasmania), offers a fascinating investigation of the theological challenges Christians had to face from the very beginning. Ochs argues that listening carefully to the voices that question and object had significant impact on the articulation of theology. In like manner, Ochs contends, fresh theological insights come from making listening to today's voices a priority. His essay, "Facing Polemics Head On: Learning Christology 'From the Side'" offers much food for thought for our own apologetic endeavours today.

Our guest speaker from Canada, Bradley M. Penner, who serves as an Instructor in Theology for Prairie College and as an adjunct faculty member for Briercrest Seminary, delves deeper into christological conundrums by investigating "The Kenotic Christology of P. T. Forsyth." P.T. Forsyth's Christology is unique amongst the plethora of opinions regarding the person and work of Jesus Christ, especially his understanding of the *kenosis* in which he believes the Son of God eternally determined himself to empty himself in the act of incarnation in Jesus Christ. Penner offers a fascinating exploration of Forsyth's focus on the moral, rather than metaphysical emptying of Jesus Christ which culminates in the crucifixion of Christ wherein God redeems humanity in this superlative moral act.

The Very Rev Andreas Loewe, Dean of Melbourne, has a special interest in combining theology and music, and especially the music of Johann Sebastian Bach. In his essay, "'Zeig uns durch deine Passion': The Christology of Bach's St John Passion," Andreas Loewe brings to life the theology of Martin Luther in the music of

J.S. Bach. I recommend reading Loewe's piece while listening to a recording of Bach's St. John Passion.

In my own contribution, which was originally presented at the Abraham Kuyper Conference in Princeton, NJ, earlier in 2016, I suggest a theological response to the contemporary refugee crisis. I focus mainly on the way this crisis has challenged Europe, and especially my homeland Germany. Dutch politician and theologian Abraham Kuyper (1837–1920) has put forward some significant arguments for Christian political engagement, which lend themselves to a powerful application in light of our refugee crisis today. I wish to challenge myself – and the reader – with this contribution and I hope that we will together grow in compassion and also concrete action with a view to alleviating the awful predicament of refugees.

Dr Michael Bräutigam
Issue Editor
Saint Nicholas Day, 2016

Pastoral Reflections on Union with Christ: Jesus' Personal, Relational Presence in the World Today

Thomas Kimber

Melbourne School of Theology

Introduction

In 2001, The National Study of Youth and Religion was initiated in the United States. Over the course of the study, more than three thousand teenagers in America have been interviewed about religion and spirituality in order to discover their beliefs about faith and practice and the influence of religion in the lives of youth. Based on the findings of this study, Christian Smith, the director of the project, describes the predominant religion among teenagers in America as "Moralistic Therapeutic Deism." There are three components that represent this common expression of belief about God and religion.

First, being a good and moral person is central to living a good and happy life. It emphasizes being nice, kind, pleasant, respectful, and responsible. Moralism in this context focuses on fulfilling one's personal potential through whatever religious path makes you feel good about yourself. Second, the purpose of religion is to feel good, happy, secure, and at peace. Smith notes, "It is about attaining subjective well-being, being able to resolve problems, and getting along amiably with other people."[1] Concepts like repentance and sin, God's sovereignty and our submission, love and grace, are not common themes. "The faith many of them have in mind effectively helps to achieve a primary life goal: to feel good and happy about oneself and one's life."[2]

Third, the participants describe their belief in a God who exists, who created the world, and even defines what it means to be moral. Yet he is distant, impersonal, and does not get involved in our affairs. While using the term "deism" the author notes, "The

---

[1] Christian Smith, "Summary Interpretation: Moralistic Therapeutic Deism," in *Soul Searching: The Religious and Spiritual Lives of American Teenagers* by Christian Smith with Melinda Lundquist Denton (Oxford: Oxford University Press, 2005), 48.

[2] Smith, "Moralistic, Therapeutic Deism," 49.

Deism here is revised from its classical eighteenth century version by the Therapeutic qualifier, making the distant God selectively available for taking care of needs."[3] The God described in this study is "not Trinitarian, he did not speak through the Torah or the prophets of Israel, was never resurrected from the dead, and does not fill and transform his people through his Spirit."[4] Not only is he distant, he is also not demanding.

Though the focus of this study is on younger Americans, the research has also found that Moral Therapeutic Deism is a "widespread, popular faith among very many U. S. adults. Our religiously conventional adolescents seem to be merely absorbing and reflecting religiously what the adult world is routinely modelling for and inculcating in its youth."[5]

In a similar study in Australia, Philip Hughes found these same themes emerging from Australian youth and adults. Participants in the study describe God as "a watcher, not a participant." God is seen as a "benevolent" being who is not demanding and "can be called on when we have particular needs." Hughes draws the connection with the U.S. study by noting that "similar themes were identified," underscoring the descriptor of Moral Therapeutic Deism.[6]

In his analysis of Western postmodernism, David Wells explores our understanding of Jesus Christ in the midst of new spiritualities, growing meaninglessness, and a world that is increasingly decentred. He summarizes that, "In Christ, men and women in all ages and cultures have found that for which the deepest impulses of the nature cry out." Yet, we live in a culture that says "what God's story should sound like rather than insisting that theology is not theology if it is not listening to God telling his own story in his own way."[7]

As a minister, my role is to help others listen to God tell his own story in his own way. Because of that, the term "deist" captures my

---

[3] Smith, 49.

[4] Smith, 50.

[5] Smith, 51.

[6] Philip Hughes, *Putting Life Together: Findings from Australian Youth Spirituality Research* (Fairfield: Fairfield Press, 2007), 142–143.

[7] David Wells, *Above All Earthly Powers: Christ in a Postmodern World* (Grand Rapids: Inter-Varsity, 2005), 7.

attention and my concern. This is the term that makes the strongest statement about the nature of God, both in who he is and in what he does. It describes a God who is distant, uncaring and unconcerned. It mistakes God's patience for apathy, God's restraint for inability, and God's discipline for meanness.

Nothing refutes the idea of a deistic God more than the person of Jesus Christ—God in flesh who came near and lived among us. Eugene Peterson reminds us: "[T]he ways Jesus goes about loving and saving the world are personal: nothing disembodied, nothing abstract, nothing impersonal. Incarnate, flesh and blood, relational, particular, local."[8]

My calling as a minister is to help others to understand and experience this truth about Jesus as Son of God and Son of Man, who is not only our Saviour, but our brother and our friend. In this regard, I would like to offer three reflections on the person of Jesus Christ in relation to pastoral work and calling. First, we must be reminded about the priority of every pastor, and that is to nurture one's own relationship with Jesus. Second, we will reflect on ministry and suffering. As ministers of the gospel, we are called to share in the sufferings of Jesus, but we are also reminded that Jesus shares in our suffering and ministers to us in our suffering. And third, we will be reminded of the essence of our calling as pastors, to keep others attentive to the presence and the work of Jesus in our midst.

The Priority of Every Pastor: Draw Near to Jesus

In his gospel, Mark offers such a simple yet profound description of the calling of the disciples. He appointed them "so that they might be with him" (3:14). Being with Jesus precedes anything and everything that the disciples would ever accomplish in the name of Jesus. It is this reality of being "with" Jesus that defines the life of the true disciple, but that is true only because it describes the very nature of Jesus himself. Isaiah prophesied that Jesus would be Immanuel, God with us. He is the God who draws near not only to his people but to all of his creation. Jesus reminds us that God does not love from a distance, but he loves up close and personal.

Throughout his ministry, Jesus invited his disciples to get away from the crowds and simply be with him. After the twelve had

---

[8] Eugene Peterson, *The Jesus Way* (Grand Rapids: Eerdmans, 2007), 1.

returned from a season of ministry, Jesus urged them to "Come away by yourselves to a desolate place and rest for a while" (Mk 6:31). In his greatest hour of agony, just before his arrest, Jesus begs the disciples, "Can you not watch with me one hour?" (Matt 26:40). But even in the face of crucifixion, Jesus promises "I will not leave you as orphans; I will come to you" (Jn 14:18). And the ultimate assurance, "I am with you always, to the end of the age" (Matt 28:20).

We must note that this nearness and "with-ness" is characteristic not only of Jesus but of his disciples as well. In Acts 4, Peter and John had just healed a crippled man, which created quite a commotion among the people. Yet, there was one overwhelming trait that the people observed about them. "Now when they saw the boldness of Peter and John, and perceived they were uneducated, common men, they were astonished. And they recognized that they had been with Jesus" (Acts 4:13). This is the one indictment brought against Peter on the night Jesus was betrayed and on trial: "This man was with him," (Matt 26:71) a servant girl declared. Peter denied it, yet it was unmistakable.

Those of us in ministry are beset by every temptation other people face. We are tempted to be spectacular and build a ministry that gains the attention of the watching world. Jesus knows what that temptation feels like. The devil took him to a high pinnacle and taunted him, "If you are the Son of God, throw yourself down from here" (Lk 4:9). Do something spectacular that will get everyone's attention. Yet, when we face this temptation, Jesus says to us, "Come away by yourself to a desolate place." Take my yoke upon you, learn from me and find rest for your soul.

We must understand that the way of Jesus is the way of solitude. But it is not a solitude of aloneness, rather it is a solitude of companionship. We enter with Jesus into the wilderness, the inner place of silence from the onslaught of voices, crowds, and opinions of this world. Solitude with Jesus is the place of transformation. It strips us of the false identities we so carefully construct in our public life. Jesus faced the solitude of the wilderness and encountered the same temptations we face. And he also strengthened and affirmed his true identity. Solitude with Jesus does the same for us. It deepens our true sense of self, created by God and for God. Apart from him we have no true self and no true life.

The way of solitude with Jesus is also the way of preparation for ministry. Our methods and our motives are purified and focused as we learn the ways of Jesus and gain the heart of Jesus. We discover the familiarity of his voice and learn the ways of his will. We learn as Jesus did that the only true motive for ministry is "to do the will of him who sent me" (Jn 5:30). In solitude, we discover that true ministry is the overflow of what Jesus is teaching me as I spend time alone with him.

In his first epistle, John draws the obvious connection between his personal encounter with Jesus and his ministry for Jesus, which he describes in the fullness of all his senses. "That which was from the beginning, which we have heard, which we have seen with our eyes, which we have looked upon and have touched with our hands... we proclaim to you" (1 Jn 1:1, 3). Henri Nouwen expresses the opinion that this will be the central question of future leaders and pastors of our time. Do we have "an ardent desire to dwell in God's presence, to listen to God's voice, to look at God's beauty, to touch God's incarnate Word and to taste fully God's infinite goodness?"[9] Our ministry must be deeply rooted and nurtured in such intimacy with Jesus, which takes us beyond the mere call to be a moral leader to being a true spiritual guide. This is where we discover as Mother Teresa observed that ministry can only be fruitful if it grows out of a direct and intimate encounter with Jesus.[10]

I have wondered for some time, as I have watched the decline of the church throughout the U.S., Europe and here in Australia, how much of the decline has come from this simple observation: Are we, indeed, abiding in Jesus and allowing Jesus to abide in us? How can we expect others to experience the nearness of Jesus if we are not experiencing and demonstrating it ourselves? To what extent have we abandoned that simple call of Jesus to "be with him," to "come away with him," and to "watch and pray with him"? What might it be like if what was said of Peter and John could be said of us, that we would be recognized as men and women who had been with Jesus?

The Experience of Pastoral Ministry: We Share in the Sufferings of Jesus

Dietrich Bonhoeffer articulated the truth that "as we embark upon discipleship we surrender ourselves to Christ in union with his

---

[9] Henri Nouwen, *In the Name of Jesus* (New York: Crossroads, 1993), 29–30.

[10] Henri Nouwen, *The Way of the Heart* (San Francisco: HarperSanFrancisco, 1991), 31.

death—we give our lives to death... When Christ calls a man, he bids him come and die."[11]   Paul expressed the same truth in Romans 6, stating that we have been united with Christ in his death, burial and resurrection. It is a union of life that comes through a union in death. If we are to share with Jesus in the love of the Father, then we must share as well in the fellowship of his suffering.

The foundations of our life and union with Christ are based in this experience of identifying with him in his death. This is the essence of our Christian identity, replacing the false identities of this world with our true, God-given identity. We must never lose sight of the truth that our identity comes through suffering. As disciples of Jesus, we are called to die daily to ourselves and share in the experience of Jesus. Jesus himself warned his disciples of the reality of this suffering. "If the world hates you, you know that it has hated me before it hated you" (Jn 15:18).

The desert fathers of the fourth and fifth centuries challenge today's thinking about a gospel of prosperity and ease. They believed that struggle is normal, even necessary and healthy for the Christian life. We cannot escape pain and struggle, neither should we try to. "Rather, we should embrace it as one aspect of our call to discipleship, for the goal of life in this world is not ease, prosperity and success but intimacy with God, maturity of character, and influence in the world. Struggle proves that we are taking the Christian faith seriously."[12]

The apostle Paul tells us that to embrace our calling as ministers means that we must also share in Jesus' experience of suffering. Because of that, he says to the Colossians, "I rejoice in my sufferings for your sake, and in my flesh I am filling up what is lacking in Christ's afflictions for the sake of his body, that is, the church" (Col 1:24). Paul's experience of suffering included imprisonments, beatings, near-death experiences, as well as the toil and hardship of missionary life. Added to the physical difficulty and inconvenience, Paul describes the emotional and relational suffering that comes through "the daily pressure on me of my

---

[11] Dietrich Bonhoeffer, *The Cost of Discipleship* (New York: MacMillan, 1963), 99.

[12] Gerald Sittser, *Water from a Deep Well: Christian Spirituality from Early Martyrs to Modern Missionaries* (Downers Grove: IVP, 2007), 74.

anxiety for all the churches. Who is weak, and I am not weak? Who is made to fall and I am not indignant?" (2 Cor 11:28–29).

But our sharing in Jesus' suffering is only possible because he took on our suffering. Isaiah prophesied that Jesus would be a man of sorrows, acquainted with grief, stricken, afflicted, abandoned and killed. As a human, Jesus experienced the full realm of suffering known to our race: Physical, emotional, psychological, relational and even spiritual suffering. And so, the writer of Hebrews tells us, Jesus presently ministers to us as a sympathetic high priest who is able to come close, not in judgment and criticism, but in grace and understanding because he feels our pain and our frustration. Only Jesus knows the full extent and power of temptation because he has felt its pull to the very limit without succumbing to sin.

This is foundational to Jesus' role as a mediator, and it is what makes his present ministry so meaningful and personal. Paul tells us in Romans 8:34 that Jesus sits at the right hand of the Father, interceding for us. It is an intercession that feels the groans and the pains of human suffering and confusion. He knows how I feel. And his awareness of my pain informs his intercession on my behalf.

So, Paul confidently declares not only do we share in Jesus' sufferings, "so through Christ we share abundantly in comfort too" (2 Cor 1:5). It is in this experience of receiving comfort from Jesus that we are empowered and enabled to minister comfort to others. As Purves observes, "There is a power for ministry in those who are themselves wounded, who have received the comfort of God, and who now minister to others in the strength of healing. The truth for pastoral work is that there is a direct relationship between woundedness, being comforted, and becoming empowered to a ministry of consolation."[13]

It is in our own suffering that we become acutely aware of the depth of our need of God. Yet, ironically, it is also in the suffering that we are tempted to question the presence of God. We have too long been wrongly convinced, as Job's sorry comforters were, that suffering is a sign of God's absence and not his presence. Yet it is in the season of suffering, the journey in the wilderness, that God draws so near we can barely discern his presence. The season in the

---

[13] Andrew Purves, *Reconstruction of Pastoral Theology* (Louisville: Westminster John Knox, 2004), 197.

wilderness is not abandonment but intimacy. Nothing enables us to share more deeply in one another's life than the mutual experience of struggle and pain, of consolation and desolation.

The Essential Calling of the Pastor: To Keep Others Attentive to Jesus

The essential calling of the pastor must follow naturally from my first two points. Pastoral ministry must be seen as the natural outflow of my life in Jesus where I learn to hear Jesus' voice and discern his ministry in my own life. As I share in his suffering, so I experience his comfort. It is only because I have experienced Jesus' personal ministry to me that I am able to minister to others.

In the present age, there are multiple demands made on pastors, many of which have little connection with pastoral calling. Indeed, with so many needs before us, how do we begin to address them all or even know which ones we can legitimately meet? Ray Anderson suggests that

> the needs of the world did not set the agenda for the ministry of Jesus. It is true that wherever the needs of the world impinged on him, he reached out to heal the sick and feed the hungry. But hunger, sickness and even death did not set the agenda for his ministry.[14]

Rather, Jesus' first priority was to serve the Father who sent him into the world. In keeping this important sense of priority, Jesus maintains proper focus on his true calling and purpose. As he says to the disciples, "I do not seek my own will but the will of him who sent me" (Jn 5:30). Even in the face of great need, Jesus' will was to accomplish the works that the Father gave him to accomplish.

In this regard, we learn much from Jesus himself about pastoral calling. Just before he was arrested, tried, and crucified, Jesus comforted his disciples with the truth that after he was gone he would send the Holy Spirit. He would not only comfort the disciples but he would help them to continue Jesus' ministry. Notably, Jesus says that the Spirit would "bring to your remembrance all that I have said to you" (Jn 14:26) and "He will glorify me, for he will take what is mine and declare it to you" (Jn 16:14). Amidst the various ministries of the Holy Spirit is this key focal point: In all he does, the Spirit does not call attention to himself; rather, he points people to Jesus Christ.

---

[14] Ray Anderson, *The Shape of Practical Theology* (Downers Grove: IVP, 2001), 41.

Eugene Peterson observes that this forms the core of the pastor's calling. Above all else, "the pastor's responsibility is to keep the community attentive to God."[15] It is unfortunate that we live in a day when we draw on Jesus' example as a moral teacher, or we draw on his influence as a historical figure. We ask ourselves questions like, "What would Jesus do if he were here?" The question makes a dangerous assumption in suggesting that Jesus is not here. But if we are to understand the biblical teaching that Jesus is presently alive and that his ministry is still vital, then we must change the question to the present reality that Jesus is here among us through the power of the Holy Spirit. As a minister, one of the most important questions I must ask of myself and of the person or people before me is this: What is Jesus doing here and now? How can I help this person before me to be attentive to the work of Christ in her life?

We live in a culture that is infatuated with celebrity. Sadly, this is true as much in the church as in society. We all face the temptation to be spectacular and make a name for ourselves. Yet, while there may be a veneer of goodness in our ministry success and notoriety, the reality too often is that all the attention is focused squarely on us. Henri Nouwen reminds us,

> Far more importantly, it is Jesus who heals, not I; Jesus who is Lord, not I. This is very clearly made visible when we proclaim the redeeming power of God together. Indeed, whenever we minister together, it is easier for people to recognize that we do not come in our own name, but in the name of the Lord Jesus who sent us.[16]

This is one of the great challenges of ministry today. Too often our focus is on building organizations that become monuments to our hard work *for* Jesus. The call of our time is to give people a glimpse of Jesus himself, who has drawn near in history and who continues to draw near through the Holy Spirit. Todd Billings reminds us,

> As ones united to Christ, we participate in the Spirit's ongoing work of bearing witness to Christ and creating a new humanity in which the dividing walls between cultures are overcome in Christ. Therefore, today's church should replace its talk of 'incarnational

---

[15] Eugene Peterson, *Working the Angles* (Grand Rapids: Eerdmans, 1987), 2.

[16] Henri Nouwen, *In the Name of Jesus*, 41.

ministry' with the more biblically faithful and theologically dynamic language of ministry as participation in Christ.[17]

Conclusion

In our day, there must be a much greater connection between our study of theology and our practice of ministry. The Bible tells us that God is personal and not distant, that we as humans have the capacity for intimacy with God, and that our calling as ministers is to help others to experience this same transforming intimacy. It requires that we become so acquainted with the ministry of Jesus described for us in Scripture and explained in our creeds that we can recognize his ministry here and now. As a minister of Jesus Christ, my calling is to nurture my own intimate life with Jesus and then to help others to experience the reality of Jesus as the healer of their soul, the healer of their relationships, the core of their identity, and the purpose for their existence. We must discover again what it means to share in God's ministry in this world, in and through the person of Jesus Christ.

---

[17] Todd Billings, *Union with Christ: Reframing Theology and Ministry for the Church* (Grand Rapids: Baker, 2011), 124.

Who Did Jesus Think He Was?
Jesus' Self-Understanding in the Synoptic Gospels

Greg Forbes

Melbourne School of Theology

Introduction

In looking at the topic *Who Did Jesus Think He Was?* we are, of course, dealing with the Christology of Jesus. It is one thing to study the Christology of Paul, the Christology of the church fathers, or the Christology of a particular theologian. However, it is another thing altogether to examine the Christology of Jesus himself.

From the perspective of a New Testament scholar such an enterprise is fraught with difficulty. There are landmines along the path, and one cannot undertake a simple walk through the Gospel terrain to glean and gather whatever may appear desirable. For lurking below the surface is the dreaded nemesis of inauthenticity. And so, anyone who wants to write on the historical Jesus, be it his teaching or deeds, must first of all deal with methodological issues.[1]

It is all too apparent that a particular view of Jesus, including what he may have thought about himself, is directly dependent upon the data under consideration. One only has to survey the material on the historical Jesus that has proliferated since 1980 to see that. So it is no real surprise that the view of Jesus presented by the Jesus Seminar, who admit 18% of the sayings material as authentic, is vastly different to that advocated by N.T. Wright, who has a much more positive approach to the Gospel data. We may well concur with Witherington's lament that some scholars do not "play with a full deck of synoptic playing cards,"[2] but that does not mean that we can introduce the full deck without some justifiable methodology.

---

[1] See Chris Forbes, "The Historical Jesus," in *The Content and Setting of the Gospel Tradition* (eds. Mark Harding and Alanna Nobbs; Grand Rapids: Eerdmans, 2010), 231–62. One of the more recent and perhaps novel approaches to methodology is that of James G. Crossley, *Jesus and the Chaos of History: Redirecting the Life of the Historical Jesus* (Oxford: Oxford University Press, 2015). Crossley suggests that other factors besides Jesus himself, such as cultural and political turmoil in Palestine and beyond, may equally explain the rise in popularity of the Jesus movement.

[2] Ben Witherington III, *The Jesus Quest: The Third Search for the Jew of Nazareth* (Downers Grove, IL: IVP, 1995), 103.

So does this bode well for a seminar on theology? I have neither the time nor the inclination in this particular setting to get bogged down in methodological procedures, yet I do feel that I am betraying my guild to some extent if I don't. So, it is going to have to suffice for the present moment to say that I am largely persuaded by James Dunn's well-argued insistence that what we have in the Synoptic Gospels is a faithful reminiscence of Jesus. In other words, the impact that Jesus made on his first followers has been preserved in the various strands of what we know as the Gospel tradition. We may not have the original words of Jesus (above all because Jesus spoke in Aramaic) but we have stories told and retold according to the norm of oral cultures. And that norm is the preservation of a core story with peripheral details varying in the telling and retelling.[3]

In any event, once the tradition is removed from the only context in which it has been transmitted anything is possible, and in fact the literature bears adequate testimony to this! So, for the moment, let us assume that Jesus' self-understanding is faithfully captured in the written Gospels. I will make some further observations on this as we proceed, and address it once more in my concluding comments.

So what then did Jesus think about himself? Obviously we do not have access to his mind, only to what has been written. So our picture will be necessarily incomplete. We must also take account not only of what Jesus said about himself but what he did, for it is true in many instances in the Gospels that actions speak louder than words. We will examine Jesus' self-understanding with respect to three areas: Messiah, Wisdom, and Son of God.

1. Messiah

a) Messiahship in first century Judaism

Messianic expectations in first century Judaism were fluid and varied, as evidenced by the popular messianic movements of the time, as well as the vast difference between, for example, the Qumran expectation of both a priestly and royal Messiah, and the Herodians who pinned their hopes on the Herodian dynasty. Nevertheless, common to most views was the expectation that the Messiah would be a catalyst for the restoration of Israel and to

---

[3] James D. G. Dunn, *Jesus Remembered. Christianity in the Making. Volume 1* (Grand Rapids: Eerdmans, 2003), 192–254. See also Dunn's third volume *Neither Jew nor Greek: A Contested Identity* (Grand Rapids: Eerdmans, 2015), 210–218.

usher in a golden age of peace and prosperity for the people of God.[4]

b) Jesus and the kingdom of God

Achieving a scholarly consensus is a rare feat in historical Jesus studies, but none deny that the kingdom of God was the focal point of Jesus' teaching. Not only was it the focal point of his teaching, but Jesus claimed that the kingdom was present in and through his ministry, and indeed himself. Because in numerous strands of Jewish thinking kingdom and Messiah went hand-in-hand,[5] the teaching of Jesus regarding the kingdom of God obviously prompted questions regarding his own identity. Thus, his citation of Isaiah 61:1–2 in Luke 4:18–19 with respect to his own ministry is not only a declaration that the kingdom is present, but can also be construed as an implicit messianic claim.

This implicit messianic claim is reinforced by his ministry proper. The miracles and exorcisms he performed align to various degrees with kingdom expectations. Building on such texts as Isaiah 35:5 and 61:1–2 and filtered through second temple messianic expectations, the prospect emerges that the Messiah would be God's agent for bringing wholeness and restoration not only to the nation but also to individuals (e.g. 4Q521). This link between kingdom, Messiah, and healing is also evident in the reply that Jesus gives to John the Baptist, who it would appear is having a certain cognitive dissonance concerning the identity of Jesus. Jesus alludes to the above-mentioned texts from Isaiah and implies that his role as the "the coming one" should be painfully obvious (Matt 11:2–5).

Drawing on Isaiah 25:6–8 the expectation developed during the second temple period of God's people participating in a great banquet in the kingdom age (cf. Matt 8:11). There are also a number of places in the literature where the Messiah was to preside over this banquet (1QSa 2:12–21; *1 Enoch* 62; cf. Mk 14:25; *2 Baruch*

---

[4] See N. T. Wright, *Jesus and the Victory of God* (London: SPCK, 1996), 481–86; Dunn, *Jesus Remembered*, 447–55; 617–22; M. F. Bird, "Christ," in *Dictionary of Jesus and the Gospels. Second Edition* (eds. Joel B. Green, Jeannine K. Brown & Nicholas Perrin; Illinois: IVP Academic, 2013), 115–25.

[5] Joel B. Green, "Kingdom of God/Heaven," in *Dictionary of Jesus and the Gospels. Second Edition* (eds. Joel B. Green, Jeannine K. Brown & Nicholas Perrin; Illinois: IVP Academic, 2013), 471–72; Stephen Voorwinde, "The Kingdom of God in the Proclamation of Jesus," in *The Content and Setting of the Gospel Tradition* (eds. Mark Harding and Alanna Nobbs; Grand Rapids: Eerdmans, 2010), 329–53.

29). Jesus' feeding of the multitudes and regular table fellowship with the marginalised should consequently be seen as a symbol and foretaste of this messianic banquet.[6] If the John 6:15 postscript to the feeding miracle has any historical credibility,[7] then the crowds obviously interpret the event messianically. Here we need not insist that Jesus rejected messianic status, only the popular conceptions of it.

c) Choosing and sending the Twelve

The selection of the Twelve places Jesus squarely in the realm of Jewish restoration eschatology. Although not many have been willing to accept N. T. Wright's Israel-still-in-exile paradigm,[8] there is not much doubt that the hopes of the nation centered on the restoration of the twelve tribes.[9] Consequently, if Jesus did not intend to imply the eschatological renewal of Israel in the selection of his disciples, then choosing twelve was a very careless choice. Wright also especially notes the choice of the inner three disciples – Peter, James, and John – which has obvious echoes of David's three mighty warriors (2 Sam 23:8–17), particularly given the association of Jesus with a Davidic royal ideology.[10]

d) Miracles

Not many scholars today, even those at the sceptical end of the spectrum, would deny that Jesus was known as a miracle worker and exorcist.[11] Most debate centres around the issue of the uniqueness of Jesus in this regard. However, to what extent such miracles were unique to Jesus is beside the point, for when interpreted against the OT background regarding the prophecies of the messianic age (Isa 35:4–6; 61:1ff), Jesus' actions must be seen as highly significant. In fact they must be construed as an implicit

---

[6] See Craig L. Blomberg, *Contagious Holiness: Jesus' Meals with Sinners* (Downers Grove, IL: IVP, 2005) for more on this topic.

[7] The obvious question remains as to why the early church might add such a statement with its obvious political overtones. See George R. Beasley-Murray, *John* (WBC; Waco: Word, 1987), 88–89.

[8] Wright, *Jesus and the Victory of God*, 198–243.

9 See B. Pitre, *Jesus, the Tribulation, and the End of the Exile: Restoration Eschatology and the Origin of the Atonement* (Grand Rapids: Baker Academic, 2005); E. P. Sanders, Jesus and Judaism (Philadelphia: Fortress, 1985); Wright, *Jesus and the Victory of God*, 299–301, 431, 532.

[10] Luke 1:32, 69; Mark 10:47; 12:35–37.

[11] See J. P. Meier, *A Marginal Jew: Rethinking the Historical Jesus. Volume Two: Mentor, Message, and Miracles* (New York Doubleday, 1994), 617–31.

messianic claim. In healing the sick, giving sight to the blind, and casting out demons[12] Jesus was proclaiming in his actions that: i) the kingdom of God was present, and ii) he was the agent of that kingdom, the messianic deliverer. This explains his otherwise enigmatic response to the question posed by John the Baptist (see above).

e) The Temple incident

For messianic expectations that embodied a royal focus (probably the dominant expectation) the temple was central. This is so because "temple and kingship went hand-in-hand."[13] The construction of the temple was planned by David and completed by Solomon, Josiah's reform was bound up with the temple (2 Kings 23), Judas Maccabaeus cleansed and rededicated the temple, Herod the Great embarked on extensive temple rebuilding, and after the time of Jesus both Simon bar Giora and Bar-Kochba performed symbolic actions regarding the temple.[14]

Although Jesus' action in the temple has been interpreted differently over the years, most nowadays regard the prime focus to be a prophetic sign of judgment regarding the temple's destruction. His behaviour did not incur immediate action by the authorities, and does not appear to be an attempt to stop the cult. Probably limited in time and space it makes more sense to regard the action as having symbolic significance, that is, a prophetic sign.

Of course this comes on the back of the manner of Jesus' entry to Jerusalem – riding an unridden colt down from the Mount of Olives. This is loaded with messianic symbolism, for Solomon, the initial son of David, was placed on the royal mule in his coronation/accession ceremony (1 Kgs 1:28–55), and the Mount of Olives carried eschatological significance given Zechariah 14:1–5. Consequently Wright, in typically understated manner, claims that "if Jesus did *not* want to be thought of in any way as Messiah, the

---

[12] Note the expectation that Satan would be vanquished at the end of the age (Isa 24:21–22; 1 Enoch 10:4ff; Jub 23:29; T. Mos 10:1; T. Levi 18:12; T. Jud. 25:3; 1QS 4:18–19; Rev 20:1–3). Thus Jesus both has supreme power (to bind Satan) and authority to inaugurate the final age of blessing.

[13] Wright, *Jesus and the Victory of God*, 483.

[14] Wright, *Jesus and the Victory of God*, 203–206, 483. Josephus (*War*, 6.283–290) also tells of a false prophet who, during the Jewish War, exhorted the people to go to the temple where they would see miraculous signs of their deliverance.

Entry and the action in the temple were extremely unwise things to undertake."[15]

f) Summary

It really makes very little sense to deny that Jesus had a messianic self-consciousness. We have only surveyed some of the relevant material here, but even that clearly points in one direction. If approximate contemporaries of Jesus (Judas the Galilean, Simon bar Giora, Bar-Kochba) could understand or portray themselves in messianic terms, and they did far less than Jesus to substantiate those claims, then why is it considered so astonishing by some that Jesus could understand himself to be the Messiah?[16]

But then, why was Jesus so reluctant to use or accept the title of *Messiah*? When the ministry of Jesus is understood against the background of Jewish messianic expectations we see that he had a far different conception of what being Messiah entailed.[17] For Jesus, the Messiah was not one to fight Israel's battle against pagan oppressors, nor was it about material prosperity and abundance, nor was it about earthly kingship. Rather, modelling himself on the Suffering Servant of Isaiah, Jesus understood his divine vocation to be to give his life as a ransom for many (Mk 10:45). Thus his messianic vocation was not triumph instead of suffering, but triumph through suffering. Given this dissonance with popular conceptions the reluctance of Jesus to accept messianic labels is quite understandable.[18]

2. Wisdom

Wisdom is one of the most enigmatic features of Jewish theology. Wisdom is not just about proper living in the sight of God, it is an aspect of God's revelation.[19] Human beings are exhorted to look at the created world around them, understand their lives as created

---

[15] N. T. Wright, "Jesus, Israel and the Cross." http://ntwrightpage.com/Wright_Jesus_Israel_Cross.pdf, Section IV. (accessed 15/06/2016) (italics retained).

[16] N. T. Wright, "Jesus, Israel and the Cross." http://ntwrightpage.com/Wright_Jesus_Israel_Cross.pdf, Section IV. (accessed 16/06/2016).

[17] See James H. Charlesworth (ed.), *The Messiah: Developments in Earliest Judaism and Christianity* (Minneapolis: Fortress Press, 1992).

[18] In this connection it is interesting to note that post-resurrection the disciples still understand the ministry of Jesus in nationalistic terms (Acts 1:6). It takes the coming of the Spirit at Pentecost to change their perceptions.

[19] In this sense most regard Wisdom as embodying general rather than specific revelation.

beings under God and order their lives appropriately. Thus wisdom can be understood as "divine truth mediated through human observation."[20]

The most relevant factor for our discussion here involves passages that personify wisdom in Proverbs and Sirach. The continuing debate concerning the origins of this personification need not delay us.[21] More relevant is the question of what Wisdom is actually personifying. Proverbs 8 indicates that Wisdom is created by God (8:22) and yet is distinct from his creation in that she was present at creation and appears to be God's agent of it (8:30; 3:19). So the relationship between Wisdom and God himself is quite enigmatic. Are we dealing here with an attribute of God poetically represented as separate transcendent being, or is Wisdom a personification of the order integral to creation itself?[22] Whereas some may consider the former an overstatement, the latter does not do total justice to the statements made about Wisdom.[23] Consequently, it does not appear to be too far a stretch to say that certain Jewish authors could conceive of Wisdom in terms of a plurality in God in a way that was not thought to compromise Jewish monotheism.

Even if some do consider this too far a stretch with respect to the original Jewish context, it obviously is not once we move into the NT material. John's Prologue and Paul certainly depict Jesus in wisdom categories, and this wisdom Christology is part of a multifaceted approach to describing the person of Jesus. However our concern here is how Jesus understood himself. So let us look at the relevant Gospel texts.

a) Matthew 11:18–19

In his defence of John the Baptist and critique of the fickleness of his contemporary generation, Jesus claims that his custom of eating and drinking with tax collectors and sinners is defensible because

---

[20] D. J. Estes, "Wisdom and Biblical Theology," in *Dictionary of the Old Testament: Wisdom, Poetry and Writings* (eds. Tremper Longman III & Peter Enns; Downers Grove, Illinois: IVP Academic, 2008), 855.

[21] See E. C. Lucas, "Wisdom Theology," in *Dictionary of the Old Testament: Wisdom, Poetry and Writings* (eds. Tremper Longman III & Peter Enns; Downers Grove, Illinois: IVP Academic, 2008), 905–906. Ben Witherington III, *Jesus the Sage: The Pilgrimage of Wisdom* (Minneapolis: Fortress Press, 1994), 3–116.

[22] Lucas, "Wisdom Theology," 905–906.

[23] Lucas, "Wisdom Theology," 906.

"wisdom is vindicated by her deeds."[24] In other words, Jesus as the Son of Man is equated with Wisdom, with the point being that as wisdom by definition cannot do anything wrong or false, Jesus' actions will ultimately vindicate him.[25]

b) Matthew 11:28–30

Here Jesus echoes the call of Wisdom in Proverbs and Sirach in summoning people to come and receive instruction (Prov 8:1–3; Sir 24:19–22; 51:23–27). Particularly relevant is Sirach 51:23–27 where Wisdom invites the uneducated to draw near and to place their neck under her yoke so that they may find serenity.

c) Matthew 12:42

In stating that "something greater than Solomon is here" Jesus is clearly referring to himself and his ministry.[26] Although Solomon was known as an exorcist in later Jewish tradition and in context of the Beelzebul controversy (vv. 22–32) the statement may be doing double duty with respect to Jesus' authority as an exorcist, the prime focus is on the wisdom of Solomon. The obvious implication is that Jesus is greater than Solomon who was the epitome of wisdom.

d) Matthean redaction and the historical Jesus

The instances cited above where Jesus speaks of himself in wisdom categories appear to go beyond a mere personification of Wisdom. Wisdom is already personified in the Jewish writings, but something greater than personification is here. These sayings suggest that Jesus understood himself to be the incarnation of Wisdom – "that Jesus presented himself both as sage and message of the sage."[27]

---

[24] This reading has early and reliable support (א B) but there is a well attested variant "by her children" that is more closely aligned with the Lucan parallel (Lk 7:35). Although "deeds" is more likely to be the original reading here in Matthew, debate still exists as to the original saying of Jesus. See Ben Witherington III, *The Christology of Jesus* (Minneapolis: Fortress Press, 1990), 51.

[25] Donald A. Hagner, *Matthew 1–13* (Word Biblical Commentary 33A; Dallas, Word, 1993), 311.

[26] The neuter πλεῖον requires the translation "something" rather than "someone." This is meant to embrace the entire ministry of Jesus as well as his person (Hagner, *Matthew 1–13*, 355).

[27] Witherington, *Jesus the Sage*, 204. Also Hagner, *Matthew 1–13*, 355; Witherington, *Christology of Jesus*, 51–53.

However, might not this be explained in terms of Matthean redaction rather than reflecting the ideas of the historical Jesus? The call of Jesus to come to him and take his yoke upon oneself is unique to Matthew, and although Matthew 12:42 has a direct parallel in Luke 11:31, this is the least explicit of the three sayings mentioned above. In addition, the Lukan parallel to Matthew 11:18–19 (Lk 7:35) reads "wisdom is vindicated by (all) her children," which need imply nothing more than Jesus and John the Baptist stand in the line of all those who have embraced wisdom. However, there is good reason to suppose that "all" is Lukan redaction,[28] and so here Jesus is likely affirming that both he and John the Baptist are the "culmination of all of Wisdom's messengers."[29]

Another relevant saying occurs in Matthew 23:34//Luke 11:49, in the context of a series of woe sayings pronounced against the scribes and Pharisees. The Lukan version reads, "Therefore the Wisdom of God also said, 'I will send prophets and apostles to them'," whereas the Matthean version has, "Therefore I send prophets and wise men and scribes to you." If Luke preserves the original saying[30] again we see that Matthew directly equates Jesus with Wisdom, and by following this immediately with the lament over Jerusalem he clearly indicates that Jerusalem is rejecting none other than Jesus as incarnate Wisdom.[31]

Although Witherington argues for the primacy of Matthew's wording in the double tradition texts,[32] most would argue that Luke more likely captures the original saying. Nevertheless, even if we follow the majority at this point it would be unwarranted to conclude that Matthew's wisdom Christology is purely the product of his own fertile theological mind. Not only are there a couple of implicit links between Jesus and Wisdom in the double tradition

---

[28] So John Nolland, *Luke 1–9:20* (Word Biblical Commentary 35a; Dallas: Word, 1989), 346.

[29] F. W. Burnett and C. Bennema, "Wisdom," in *Dictionary of Jesus and the Gospels. Second Edition* (eds. Joel B. Green, Jeannine K. Brown & Nicholas Perrin; Illinois: IVP Academic, 2013), 996.

[30] So John Nolland, *Luke 9:21–18:34* (Word Biblical Commentary 35b; Dallas: Word, 1993), 667; I. Howard Marshall, *Commentary on Luke* (NIGTC; Grand Rapids: Eerdmans, 1978), 502.

[31] F. W. Burnett and C. Bennema, "Wisdom," 998; Donald A. Hagner, *Matthew 14–28* (Word Biblical Commentary 33b; Dallas: Word, 1995), 675.

[32] Witherington, *Christology of Jesus*, 49–52.

sayings source, there is a strong wisdom Christology present in both John and Paul. Consequently, it would appear that a wisdom Christology is not a later theological development in the early church, but was present from early times. Not only this, it is present throughout the various strata of the NT. Consequently, it is likely that the seeds of this wisdom Christology were planted by Jesus himself, and taken up by the NT writers as an appropriate and at-hand category to use in their multifaceted Christology.

In this connection it is also instructive to note the affinities between the ministry of Jesus and the career of Wisdom. Wisdom has a unique relationship with and proximity to God (Sir 24:1–6), is the pre-existent agent of creation (Prov 8:22–31), grants life (Prov 8:35), is linked to truth (Prov 8:7) and the word of God (Sir 24:3), dwells among the people of God in Jerusalem (Sir 24:8–12), gives revelation and instruction, and after suffering rejection returns to God in heaven (1 Enoch 42).

In conclusion then, Jesus spoke of himself in wisdom categories and laid the foundation for a developing wisdom Christology whereby he would be not only be portrayed as personified Wisdom but Wisdom incarnate.

3. Son of God

Given the OT and ANE usage, the use of this title in and of itself is ambiguous and inconclusive. We will briefly outline the Jewish usage as this provides the prime background for the ministry of Jesus.

a) "Son of God" in the Old Testament and Judaism

In the plural, "sons of God" could be used of angelic beings (Prayer of Joseph 1:6–7; Gen 6:1–2 [possibly]), and was also a covenant term depicting Israel as the elect people of God (Ex 4:22; Hos 11:1). In the singular, it was used of Jewish miracle workers such as Hanina Ben Dosa,[33] but the most significant usage for our purposes relates to Jewish kings, especially David and his descendants in terms of the Father–son relationship expressed in the covenant of 2 Samuel 7:13–14. This *functional* usage is not to be understood in terms of divine sonship as evident in Greco-Roman culture and

---

[33] Hanina ben Dosa is addressed as "my son" by a (presumably divine) voice from Mount Horeb (*b. Ber.* 17b).

religion,³⁴ but represented the mediation of God's rule through the king and the intimate relationship the king enjoyed as recipient and heir of God's blessing.

The linking of son of God terminology with Davidic kingship led naturally to the linking of son of God and Messiah. With the discovery of the Qumran texts clear evidence is now at hand that this correspondence was made in Second Temple Judaism,³⁵ although how widespread this was is unclear. Nevertheless, the possibility remains that both Peter's confession, "You are the Messiah, the Son of the living God" (Matt 16:16), and the question of the high priest "Are you the Messiah, the Son of the Blessed One?" (Matt 26:63) are not two separate statements/questions, but one.

So, in Jewish thought at the time of Jesus "son of God" was not a divine title, and could be used to designate a number of specific functional relationships between human beings and God, including that of Messiah.

b) The term "Son of God" in the Synoptic Gospels

In Luke's Infancy Narratives the angel Gabriel announces to Mary that her son would be called the "Son of God" (Lk 1:35). This proves to be the case but from somewhat unexpected sources. Those who call Jesus by this title are: i) the narrator of Luke and Mark (Mk 1:1; Lk 3:38); ii) the voice from heaven at Jesus' baptism (Mk 1:11 and par.), iii) Satan in the temptation narratives (Matt 4:3,6; Lk 4:3,9 – by means of a conditional statement), iv) demons (Mk 3:11 and par.), v) the high priest in the form of a question (Mk 14:61; Matt 26:63), vi) those who mock Jesus on the cross (Matt 27:40), vii) Matthew's version of Peter's confession (Matt 16:16), viii) the disciples after they saw Jesus walk on water (Matt 14:33), and ix) the Roman centurion in light of the death of Jesus (Mk 15:39; Matt 27:55). Only the final three are confessions of human beings in a positive sense, although we have already seen above that

---

³⁴ Whereas the Greeks could ascribe divine sonship to a living human being (e.g. Plato), the Romans reserved this status mainly for deceased emperors. A living emperor could be termed "son of God," in the sense that he was descended from one who was now deified. See A. Winn, "Son of God" in *Dictionary of Jesus and the Gospels. Second Edition* (eds. Joel B. Green, Jeannine K. Brown & Nicholas Perrin; Illinois: IVP Academic, 2013), 887.

³⁵ 4Q174. There are a couple of other possible references in the Scrolls (4Q246, 1Q28a, 4Q369) but due to the fragmentary nature of the text these are less certain. See Winn, "Son of God," 886–87. The apocalyptic book *4 Ezra* also links "son" with Messiah.

Peter's confession was most likely more about messiahship than divine sonship. The confession of the Roman centurion serves a literary and theological function in Mark and even if the event was historical it is difficult to construe what the soldier meant by this statement. This leaves only Matthew 14:33. Yet even here, it is not necessary that the disciples understood Jesus to be God incarnate, but rather one sent from God with unique authority and power (i.e., his messianic agent).[36]

But what relevance is this to a study of the Christology of Jesus? After all, we are examining what Jesus understood with respect to his own person, not what others thought of him. The significance lies in the fact that Jesus did not use the term "Son of God" of himself. There is no doubt whatsoever in Gospel scholarship that Jesus' preferred self-designation was "Son of Man," and this was so as a way of avoiding popular misconceptions regarding Messiah.[37] Nevertheless, there are a limited number of sayings in the Synoptics where Jesus refers to himself as simply "the Son," and all of these seem to imply "Son of God" rather than "Son of Man." We will examine each of these in turn:

i) The Johannine thunderbolt (Matt 11:27//Luke 10:22)

This is an extraordinary saying, not only because it transports the reader into the world of John's Gospel, it also represents "one of the highest points of synoptic Christology."[38] The relationship that Jesus describes here is not only intimate but unique in the sense of shared knowledge and delegation of authority. No doubt this saying explains to a large extent Jesus' conception of *abba* (see below). That is, he is God's unique son.

ii) The Parable of the Wicked Tenants (Mk 12:1–12 par.)

Not only is this parable true to life in first century Palestine, it should also be considered authentic due to the fact that the parable ends with the death of the son and the details of his death do not

---

[36] So Hagner, Matthew 24–28, 424–25. The fact that the disciples "worshiped him" also need not imply an understanding of divinity. The verb προσκυνέω is used a number of times in Matthew of paying homage (2:2, 8, 11), or of a state of humility when someone requests that Jesus act on their behalf (8:2; 9:18; 15:25).

[37] There is a significant debate regarding the linguistic background to Jesus' use of "Son of Man." See D. Burkett, *The Son Of Man Debate: A History and Evaluation* (SNTSMS 107; Cambridge: Cambridge University Press, 1999).

[38] Hagner, *Matthew 1–13*, 318.

match historically with the crucifixion.[39] If Jesus is alluding to himself as the "beloved son" (12:6) then he also claims to be heir of the vineyard. Given passages such as Isaiah 5:1–7 the Jewish audience would most naturally identify the vineyard with Israel and the owner with God. Again we are presented with a father-son relationship that appears to be deeper than functional.

iii) The Time of the End (Mk 13:32 par)

Based on the criterion of embarrassment this is one of the least disputed sayings of Jesus. Even though surrounded by Son of Man sayings the linking with "the Father" most likely indicates that "Son" should be taken in the sense of Son of God. The saying implies that even though the knowledge of the Son is limited, it is still superior to human knowledge.

iv) The Great Commission (Matt 28:19)

The triadic formula itself "in the name of the Father and of the Son and of the Holy Spirit" is likely redactional, with the original saying probably reading "in my name." This would align with early Christian preaching (represented in Acts) where new converts were baptized *in the name of Jesus*.[40] Even so, this saying should be considered as part of the collective evidence for Jesus' understanding of his unique sonship, especially given his recognition that "all authority in heaven and on earth has been given to me."

c) Other synoptic texts that inform Jesus as Son of God

Although the synoptic texts where Jesus speaks of himself as Son (of God) are limited, there is more evidence to be considered. A person's self-understanding is not only reflected explicitly in what they say concerning themselves, but implicitly in their wider speech and conduct. Consequently, we need to examine other claims, statements, and actions attributed to Jesus.

i) Mark 2:1–10 and par.

Although this is a Son of Man saying, in pronouncing forgiveness of the paralysed man's sins Jesus is claiming divine prerogatives. The response of the Jewish authorities is predictably an allegation of

---

[39] Craig A. Evans, *Mark 8:27–16:20* (Word Biblical Commentary 34b; Nashville: Thomas Nelson, 2001), 530–33, 536.

[40] Robert. H. Gundry, *Matthew: A Commentary on His Handbook for a Mixed Church under Persecution*. Second Edition (Grand Rapids: Eerdmans, 1994), 596; Hagner, *Matthew 14–28*, 887–88.

blasphemy. This presumption of access to the divine law courts is again made implicitly in the parable of the Tax Collector and Pharisee, where Jesus issues the surprising pronouncement that the tax collector returns home justified rather than the Pharisee (Lk 18:9–14).

ii) Abba (Mk 14:36)

Mark records the address of Jesus to God in the garden of Gethsemane in both transliterated Aramaic (Αββα) and Greek translation of the Aramaic ὁ πατηρ (father). Jeremias influenced a subsequent generation of scholars in contending that the Aramaic term was one of unparalleled intimacy and was equivalent to use of "daddy" by a young child. Jesus was doing something entirely new.[41] However, this has since shown to be an overstatement. There is evidence from the Qumran scrolls of God being petitioned as father using this form of address,[42] and other Jewish literature indicates that adult children addressed their fathers in this way, not just young children.[43] Nevertheless, the address by Jesus is distinctive and obviously made an impression on his followers. First of all, this is seen in the fact that the Aramaic is preserved in the tradition. This is not a common tendency and indicates some measure of the extraordinary. The natural assumption would be that this was remembered as Jesus' habitual mode of addressing God. Second, we find Paul encouraging believers as adopted children of God to address him as "Abba, Father" (Rom 8:15–16; Gal 4:6). Given that this results from a new status of reconciliation with God, it is to be understood as both a position of privilege, and therefore a title of intimacy. This is underlined by the fact that believers participate in this relationship on the basis of sharing in the sonship of Jesus.[44] Indeed, it is the Spirit of his Son at work in the hearts of believers that prompts them to address God in this way.

iii) "My" kingdom

There are a couple of isolated sayings in Matthew where Jesus speaks of his own kingdom. This prompts the obvious question as to the relationship between the kingdom of Jesus and the kingdom of

---

[41] J. Jeremias, *The Prayers of Jesus* (London: SCM, 1967), 96.

[42] 4Q372 1.16; 4Q460 5.6

[43] Robert H. Stein, *Mark* (BECNT; Grand Rapids: Baker Academic, 2008), 662.

[44] See Dunn, *Jesus Remembered,* 715–718; Evans, *Mark 8:27–16:20,* 412–13.

God. There is also the angelic announcement to Mary in Luke 1:33 in connection with him being called "the Son of the Most High" and ruling over the house of Jacob that "there will be no end to *his kingdom*."

In terms of the birth announcement, the Davidic imagery and messianic implications tend to steer our understanding in the direction of Jesus being God's vice-regent in ruling over his kingdom. Thus we should avoid the notion of the kingdom of Jesus being a this-worldly, temporal/historical reign as opposed to God's kingdom being other-worldly and beyond history.

With respect to the two sayings in Matthew, the first occurs in an eschatological context as Jesus explains the Parable of the Weeds (Matt 13:36–43). At the end of the age the angels will purge all evil and causes of sin from *the kingdom of the Son of Man*. The righteous then "will shine like the sun in the kingdom of their Father." Jesus has previously explained that the field where the seed is sown corresponds to the world (v. 38), and so logically it would appear that there is some correspondence between the world and the kingdom of Son of Man.[45] It is possible that the kingdom of Jesus is pictured here as God's reign on earth exercised through the Son in the present age. However, as we are in the world of parable we need to be careful about drawing firm conclusions from malleable language.

The second saying in Matthew (16:28) gives a different perspective. Here, the kingdom of the Son of Man is still future and is bound up with his return in glory and dispensing of judgment. The fact that he "comes with his angels in the glory of his Father" (v. 27) tends to militate against rigid separation between the kingdom of God and the kingdom of the Son of Man.

So in these isolated sayings we find casual references to a kingdom that belongs to Jesus. The kingdom is evident in the current age, yet has a future dimension and is eternal in nature. The relationship of this kingdom to the kingdom of God is not clearly defined, yet the clarity and assuredness of his own kingship and reign at the very least informs directly on his messianic self-understanding and quite probably on the understanding of his relationship to the Father as Son. In other words, it is an outflow of his unique relationship with God that he can share in the rule of the kingdom with the Father. It

---

[45] So Hagner, *Matthew 1–13*, 394.

may well be that the tradition that recalled Jesus speaking of his own kingdom provided the impetus for Paul to speak of believers being "rescued from the power of darkness and being transferred into the kingdom of his beloved Son" (Col 1:13).

d) Conclusion

We are on reasonably firm ground in believing that Jesus did speak of his relationship to God in terms of Son-Father. Although nowhere using the title *Son of God* himself, it is implied in a couple of texts and informed by several others. What is less clear is how Jesus construed this relationship. It clearly goes beyond a functional usage found in the OT and other Jewish writings, yet Jesus does not elaborate on his person in terms of a Nicene and post-Nicene Christology. As Dunn states, "The Nicene Creed represents the crystallization of a process stretching over nearly three centuries. Our concern here is with the *beginning* of that process."[46] I am also aware that we have not examined the Gospel of John in our discussion, but clearly there the Father-Son relationship is understood in terms of deity. Jesus implies this more strongly in the Fourth Gospel, and John states it directly in his opening verse.

So what can we say? Beyond doubt Jesus had an unparalleled sense of his own authority as one sent by God and the understanding of the relationship that he shared with God was distinctive and one of shared intimacy. This relationship was such that he assumed divine prerogatives and expected to participate in God's sovereign rule. I again cite Dunn:

> Only if this were the case would the Fourth Gospel's massive expansion and elaboration of the Father-Son theme have been as justifiable in tradition-historical terms; and only so would the other elaborations and developments of the Son-christology have been as acceptable as in the event they proved to be.[47]

Summary and Conclusion

It strains credibility to argue that Jesus did not reflect much on his own person, did not have a messianic self-consciousness, and that the Christology contained in the Gospels is purely the result of later church reflection. This type of thinking, rather than representing

---

[46] Dunn, *Jesus Remembered*, 708 (italics retained).

[47] Dunn, *Jesus Remembered*, 724.

"critical virility,"[48] owes more to a paranoid skepticism that wants to present an inoffensive Jesus that is conducive to the (post) modern mind. And so, rather than operating from a claimed position of objective neutrality, large swathes of Gospel texts are rejected on an *a priori* basis.[49] The vicious circle is not a playground reserved solely for the scholarly right.

Much more likely, the christological reflection of the NT writers and the early church, rather than originate from a well-meaning desire to portray their leader in lofty terms, arose directly as a result of the impact that Jesus had upon them. The disciples remembered that Jesus spoke in exclusive terms regarding his relationship with God, they remembered that he taught and acted from an unquestionable sense of authority, and they remembered that he attached prime importance to his mission.[50] The logic of history demands a close link between the historical Jesus and the proclaimed Christ.[51]

Finally, and flowing on from the above, when examining the Christology of Jesus it is not simply a case of looking at isolated sayings or pericopes in the Gospels and judging their authenticity or otherwise. We need to look at the tradition as a whole. The impression that Jesus made upon his followers does not come from isolated sayings, but from a life lived out among his disciples over an extended period. Jesus was not a talking head; he was a charismatic figure who was remembered as doing extraordinary things and teaching about the kingdom of God in vivid and confronting ways. Hence, Dale Allison is surely correct in arguing that if we cannot trust the overall impression of the Jesus tradition, then we can be sure of nothing at all regarding Jesus.[52] And I have argued in this paper that the overall impression we gain from the

---

[48] The phrase is from Dunn, *Neither Jew nor Greek*, 58.

[49] The Jesus Seminar being an obvious case in point. For a critique, see Witherington, *The Jesus Quest*, 42–57; Wright, *Jesus and the Victory of God*, 28–35; Darrell L. Bock, "The Words of Jesus in the Gospels: Life, Jive, or Memorex?" in *Jesus under Fire: Modern Scholarship Reinvents the Historical Jesus* (eds. Michael J. Wilkins & J. P. Moreland; Grand Rapids: Zondervan, 1995), 73–99.

[50] Dunn, *Jesus Remembered*, 705–707.

[51] Paul W. Barnett, *Jesus and the Logic of History* (New Studies in Biblical Theology No. 3; Leicester: Apollos, 1997), 34–35.

[52] Dale C. Allison, *Jesus of Nazareth: Millenarian Prophet* (Minneapolis: Fortress, 1998).

Synoptics is that Jesus had a messianic self-awareness, that he understood himself as the embodiment of Wisdom, and that he was the Son of God in a unique and intimate sense.

Your Kingdom Come, Your Will Be Done: An Analysis of Matthew 6:10

Andrew Mitchell

Melbourne School of Theology

Introduction

Over recent decades, the consensus interpretation of the second and third petitions of the Lord's Prayer has played a part in shaping our understanding of the "kingdom of God." The second petition is often understood *both* as a prayer for the coming of the eschatological kingdom *and* for the kingdom to grow in some sense. The third petition is typically understood as a prayer for increase in obedience to God's will. They are often linked together as more or less synonymous, with the third petition (your will be done) being used as an explanation of the second (your kingdom come).

For example, R.T. France writes: "The third of these clauses builds on the second: the essence of the coming of God's kingship is that he is duly obeyed and his purpose fulfilled."[1] Similarly J.M. Stubblefield: "The third petition urges, 'Thy will be done' (Matt 6:10). It is an explication of the preceding one. The kingdom of God is actualized whenever his perfect will is accomplished."[2] Missiologists Van Rheenen and Parker explain: "The Lord's Prayer gives the most fundamental definition of kingdom in all Scripture… The phrase 'kingdom of God' is thus defined by the Lord's Prayer as 'God's will being done on earth as it is in heaven.'"[3]

However, attention has not been paid to the semantic range of the language used, nor to the use of the third petition elsewhere in the NT. It is the intention of this article to examine Matthew 6:10

---

[1] R.T. France, *The Gospel of Matthew* (The New International Commentary on the New Testament, Grand Rapids: Eerdmans 2007), 246.

[2] J.M. Stubblefield, "Matthew 6:5–15" in *Review and Expositor* 87 (1990), 305.

[3] G. Van Rheenen and A. Parker, *Missions: Biblical Foundations and Contemporary Strategies* (Grand Rapids: Zondervan, 2014), 72–73. Note also Scot McKnight: "These two requests are to be read together: God's Kingdom coming means God's will being done on earth." (*One.Life: Jesus Calls, We Follow* [Grand Rapids: Zondervan, 2010], 32.) Tom Wright argues, "remember that 'the kingdom,' once again, is not 'heaven,' but the state of affairs in which God's kingdom has come, and his will is being done, *on earth* as in heaven." (*Virtue Reborn* [London: SPCK, 2010], 101.)

particularly with these considerations in mind. In doing so we will find that the typical interpretation can no longer be supported. Rather, the second petition is a prayer for the eschatological ushering in of the kingdom. It cannot have the sense of a gradual coming of the kingdom. The third petition is a prayer that God's sovereign purposes come about. It is not, as is often suggested, a prayer for the increase in obedience to God's will.

Context

The Lord's Prayer consists of seven phrases, the first addressing God the Father in heaven, followed by six petitions. The first three petitions are concerned with God himself: that his name is sanctified, his kingdom come, and his will be done. The latter three, however, are personal requests asking for provision (bread for the day), forgiveness of sin, and deliverance from the evil one. The prayer is part of the Sermon on the Mount (Matthew 5–7) which D.A. Carson summarises as being "concerned with entering the Kingdom."[4]

Petition Two: Your Kingdom Come

Βασιλεία σου (your kingdom) speaks of the immense reality of God's kingdom. While much could be said here, it is sufficient for our purposes to say that the kingdom is the long-awaited intervention by God to gather and save his people, bringing justice, judgment and restoration. The kingdom had come, in a sense, when Jesus entered the scene as king (e.g. Matt 12:28; Lk 17:21). Obviously, this is not what Jesus is praying for here. There are two perspectives held by commentators: the eschatological interpretation, and the gradual interpretation.

Eschatological interpretation

First, the eschatological interpretation simply refers to the kingdom which is to come in the future when Jesus shall return and the new

---

[4] D.A. Carson, *The Sermon on the Mount* (Carlisle: Paternoster Press, 1994), 14. This is indicated at various points by its structure and contents. First, that the beatitudes begin and end with the declaration "theirs is the kingdom of heaven" (5:3,10–12). Second, the statements immediately before the body of the sermon, "unless your righteousness exceeds that of the scribes and Pharisees, you will never enter the kingdom of heaven" (5:21). Then the conclusion begins, "Enter by the narrow gate." (7:13). The fact that the kingdom is in view here is further confirmed shortly after when Jesus says "Not everyone who says to me, 'Lord, Lord,' will enter the kingdom of heaven, but the one who does the will of my Father" (7:21). In fact, this question of who will enter the Kingdom dominates the entire conclusion in 7:13–27.

age begins. This is not suggesting that the kingdom was not present in Christ, but simply that this petition expresses a longing for that final day and prays for its arrival.

The eschatological interpretation is virtually undisputed for the following reasons.[5] First, while the kingdom is never the subject of the verb "to come" outside the Gospels, the idea of God, or his day of salvation "coming" is a major theme in the OT and other Jewish writing.[6] Nolland, therefore, suggests "the petition is readily understood as a reformulation in kingdom language of the OT anticipation of the coming of God in judgment and salvation."[7]

Second, the second petition's similarity to other Jewish prayers for the kingdom suggests an eschatological focus. In fact, some argue that "the first part of the Lord's Prayer can be understood directly as a summary of the Qaddish."[8] This is perhaps overstating the connection, since there is no certainty this version of the Qaddish was used in the first century. Nevertheless, the fact that "the coming reign of God is frequently prayed for in Jewish prayers"[9] adds weight to the eschatological interpretation.[10]

---

[5] E.g. France, *Matthew*, 246: "perhaps the most clearly futuristic reference to God's kingdom in Matthew."

[6] L. Morris, *The Gospel according to Matthew* (Grand Rapids: IVP, 1992), 145–6; D.C. Allison, W.D. Davies, *The Gospel According To Saint Matthew Volume I* (Edinburgh: T & T. Clark, 1988), 604–5. See, for example, Mal 4:1.

[7] J. Nolland, *The Gospel of Matthew: A Commentary on the Greek Text* (Grand Rapids: Eerdmans, 2005), 289.

[8] U. Luz, *Matthew 1–7* (translated by W.C. Linss, Edinburgh: T&T Clark, 1989), 379; Davies & Allison, *Matthew*, 606–7; C.S. Keener, *The Gospel of Matthew* (Grand Rapids: Eerdmans, 2009), 219–220. The Qaddish begins: "May His great Name grow exalted and sanctified in the world that He created as He willed. May He give reign to His kingship in your lifetimes and in your days."

[9] Luz, *Matthew*, 377–78.

[10] We might add to this the fact that Matthew's prayer is found in full in the Didache. There are two other references to the kingdom which are both clearly eschatological. This suggests an eschatological hope was the likely understanding of the kingdom petition.

Furthermore, a third argument is sometimes mounted that this eschatological hope is believed to be the idea behind the first three petitions as a whole. Since the fullest manifestation of all three requests (however they may be understood), is found in the consummated kingdom, then this is likely to be the emphasis of all three petitions. Turner, for example, suggests: "To a certain extent, God's character is revered as he rules on earth through people who do his will, but the main focus of these requests is on the future full manifestation of God's reign on earth." He therefore concludes that "the three 'your' requests should be understood as three ways of asking for essentially the same thing." D.L. Turner, *Matthew* (Baker Exegetical Commentary on the NT, Grand Rapids: Baker Academic, 2008), 186; C.H. Talbert, *Matthew*

Gradual interpretation

However, the second petition is often understood as requesting that the kingdom continues to come or to increase through this present age. This *gradual* interpretation is often upheld alongside the eschatological interpretation.

The basis for the gradual interpretation can be categorised into the following three arguments. First, a gradual coming of the kingdom is implied by the fact that the kingdom is already present. France suggests, for example, that "this petition is not so much asking that something may become true which is not true already (that God may become king) but rather that his actual kingship de jure may be fully implemented de facto as people submit to his sovereignty."[11] Or Gundry: "Jesus taught a present coming of God's rule (see esp. 12:28; Lk 11:20)... [which] suggest[s] a prayer that at the present time more people become children of God through taking on themselves the yoke of discipleship and so do the will of God on earth as it is done in heaven."[12]

Second, the gradual interpretation is supported by the content of the third petition ("your will be done"). As Dillon explains: "With the added phrase, 'thy will be done on earth as in heaven,' the necessity of active human cooperation in God's triumph is expressed *by way of interpretation* of 'thy Kingdom come.'"[13] Or as Stubblefield puts it: "The third petition... is *an explication* of the preceding one. The kingdom of God is actualized whenever his perfect will is accomplished."[14]

(Grand Rapids: Baker Academic, 2010), 89. Garland likewise sees the three themes interwoven together throughout the OT, for example in Zechariah: "And the Lord will become king over all the earth; on that day, YHWH will be one, and His name will be one" (Zech 14:9). D.E. Garland, "The Lord's prayer in the gospel of Matthew" in *Review and Expositor* 89 (1992), 219. Davies and Allison also point out that the same construction of the first three petition (that of aorist imperative + article + subject + σου) suggests "common content." As does the fact that "'on earth as it is in heaven' could fittingly be subjoined to each." (Davies & Allison, *Matthew*, 603–04.)

[11] France, *Matthew*, 246.

[12] R.H. Gundry, *Matthew, A Commentary on His Literary and Theological Art* (Grand Rapids: Eerdmans, 1982), 106. C.f. Turner, *Matthew*, 186–7; A.I. Wilson, "The Disciples' prayer: A fresh look at a familiar text" in *RTR* 57 (1998), 144.

[13] R.J. Dillon, "On the Christian Obedience of Prayer (Matthew 6:5–13)" in *Worship* 59 (1985), 421.

[14] Stubblefield, *Matthew 6:5–15*, 305. See also France, *Matthew*, 246: "The third of these clauses builds on the second: the essence of the coming of God's kingship is that he is duly obeyed and his purpose fulfilled."

This is not at odds with an eschatological viewpoint. For, as Davies and Allison suggest, "if one sincerely prays for the realization of certain eschatological hopes, the present cannot but be implicated."[15] The second and third petitions are, in a sense, co-interpretive and thereby demonstrate the "already-not yet" of the kingdom.

Third, a purely eschatological view of the coming kingdom is seen as being at odds with Matthew's agenda in the Sermon on the Mount where his focus is on the obedience of the disciple. So, as Dillon explains, "Matthew's repeated emphasis, in the Sermon on the Mount and elsewhere, is upon bringing Christian conduct into harmony with the gifts received in Christ… expressing the ingredient of human obedience to God's rule as prerequisite for the final consummation."[16] France suggests: "To view these three petitions as purely eschatological is to defuse one of the most demanding prayers disciples can be called on to offer, with far-reaching consequences for the daily conduct of our lives."[17]

Analysis

There are problems, however, with the gradual interpretation. The second petition is for the kingdom to "come" (ἐλθέτω: aorist, active, imperative of ἔρχομαι). The verb ἔρχομαι simply means "to come" or "to go." The emphasis is on the arrival and contrasts with the ideas of increasing, growing, etc. which are required for the gradual interpretation. This coming "often has the sense of appearing, of coming forward publicly, of coming on the scene. It is often used of decisive events, of happenings, of natural phenomena."[18]

Likewise, as already mentioned, it is used with theological significance for the coming of God, angels, salvation, or Jesus himself. Jesus often stated his own purposes on earth using ἔρχομαι/ἦλθον sayings (Mk 1:38; 2:17; Lk 5:32; 12:49; Matt 5:17;

---

[15] Davies & Allison, *Matthew*, 606–07.

[16] Dillon, *Prayer*, 421–22.

[17] R. France, *The Gospel According to Matthew, An Introduction and Commentary* (Grand Rapids: Eerdmans, 1985), 134. He goes on: "[T]o view them as purely ethical is to ignore the 'blessed hope' which is the mainspring of New Testament discipleship."

[18] G. Kittel, G.W. Bromiley, and G Friedrich, (Eds.), *Theological dictionary of the New Testament* (Grand Rapids: Eerdmans: 1964), 667 (hereafter referred to as TDNT).

10:34).[19] It is also used in describing the coming and going of ages, the day of salvation or judgment, and, in the NT, the coming of the kingdom. Under such circumstances the sense is of something coming to pass, or coming in time. Therefore, it is the *arrival* of something theologically significant in view. It does not have the sense of increase or growth or gradual change over time.

We can easily see a contrast with the verbs used in the parables of growth (e.g. Mk 4:26–32) where we do not find ἔρχομαι. It is also noteworthy that in the phrases of motion or proximity associated with the kingdom, ἔρχομαι seems to be used predominantly (if not exclusively) with respect to the final coming of the kingdom (see Mk 9:1; 11:10; Lk 11:2; 17:20; 22:18).[20] This contrasts both with the announcement and offer of the kingdom to the crowds where ἐγγίζω ("at hand", Mk 1:15; Lk 10:9,11; Matt 3:2; 4:17; 10:7) is always used, and with the statements of the presence of the kingdom where φθάνω ("come upon", Matt 12:28; Lk 11:20) or ἐντὸς ὑμῶν ἐστιν ("is in the midst of you", Lk 17:21) are used.[21]

"Your kingdom come" is a petition for just such an event and time to arrive. This alone seems to disqualify the gradual interpretation because it requires ἔρχομαι to mean something that it cannot mean. When one speaks of "progressive actualization," or "implementation as people submit to God's rule" or the like, it is not "kingdom *come*" they are speaking of. For that, a different verb would be required.

Moreover, it is significant that the aorist imperative is used here. Typically, the "aorist imperative serves to indicate *that* something is to be done, whereas the present imperative specifies how or when something is to be done."[22] An aorist is simply a statement and

---

[19] This is in line with its use in the wider culture, particularly in magical traditions, where a deity would be requested to come to someone's aid. TDNT, 667. Speaking of the two instances in Matt 5:17, Morris suggests: "*I came* is a significant expression; it is not one that a person would normally use of himself. It will have a meaning like 'came into the world,' 'came from God' and points to a consciousness of mission." Morris, *Matthew*, 107.

[20] Note, it seems correct to include the cries of the crowds and the question of the Jews since their expectation would certainly have been of a one-time arrival of the kingdom.

[21] It is noteworthy that in response to the Jews' question in Luke 17 about the coming (ἔρχομαι) of the kingdom, we do not find Jesus using ἔρχομαι. Instead another phrase is employed. This suggest that the "ἔρχομαι of the kingdom" may be associated with its fulfilment.

[22] D.A. Black, *Learn to Read New Testament Greek* (Nashville: B&H, 2009), 186.

often, though not exclusively, refers to a one-time event rather than an ongoing process. This fits well with the eschatological interpretation and creates a problem for the gradual view.

Furthermore, an eschatological view does not contradict the idea that the kingdom arrived in Jesus. For example, in Luke 17:20ff the Pharisees ask Jesus "when the kingdom of God would come." He responded by saying "the kingdom of God is (present tense) in the midst of you." But immediately afterwards he speaks to his disciples of his second coming. Importantly, it is to those who recognised the kingdom's presence in his first coming who, alone, were told the details of his, and the kingdom's, final and ultimate coming at the parousia.[23] This passage also reveals the events in Jesus' mind with respect to the "coming" of the kingdom. It is connected with the definitive acts of his first and second coming.

The setting of this prayer within the Sermon on the Mount, contrary to Dillon and others, actually brings this future kingdom more into focus. Not only is entry into the kingdom the great theme, but the context of that entry is the final judgment and the age to come (see particularly 5:20; 7:12–13, 22–23).[24]

Furthermore, the association between obedience and a gradual increase of the kingdom is not clearly stated in the Sermon on the Mount.[25] Instead, obedience is commanded for the very purpose of *allowing entry* into the kingdom (see 5:20 and 7:21). This eschatological entry into the kingdom is the overarching concern of the Sermon on the Mount, and is therefore the likely context for the saying "your kingdom come" within it.[26]

---

[23] As Bock says: "The kingdom may be in the midst, but its presence does not mean that the day of the Son of Man's glorious coming has occurred. So Jesus now turns to the theme of his return, which will bring about the kingdom's consummation." D. L. Bock, *Luke: 9:51–24:53* (Grand Rapids: Baker Academic, 1996), 1420.

[24] Note 7:22 "on that day," and the illustrations of 7:24–27 implies a warning of ultimate judgment.

[25] In fact, a survey of the verbs associated with the kingdom in Matthew shows the following: Enter: 5:20; 7:21; 18:3; 19:23–24; 21:31; 23:13. Proclaim/hear: 4:23; 9:35; 10:7; 13:19; 24:14. Possession (is/belongs): 5:3,10; 19:14. Recline at table: 8:11. Seek: 6:33. Know: 13:11. Shine in: 13:43. Trained for: 13:52. Give keys for: 16:19. Inherit: 25:34.

[26] Notice also that the events which will finally and completely usher the kingdom in are central throughout Matthew (e.g. 8:11; 13:47–50; 24:29ff; 26:29). That reality, and the events which will usher it in, are not dependant on human activity. In fact, quite the opposite is true. Jesus warns the disciples, "Therefore you also must be ready, for the Son of Man is coming at an hour you do not expect" (Matt 24:44). This is followed by three stories warning the

With these problems for the gradual interpretation noted, the second petition seems to be eschatological in nature. It is a prayer for the coming of Christ and the ushering in of the eschatological kingdom. It is unlikely to have added connotations of a progressive coming of the kingdom. Rather, it has the decisive, one time, future event in view.

Petition Three: Your Will Be Done

The noun θέλημα (will) refers to that which one wishes to happen, or what is willed or desired. In Matthew, θέλημα is used exclusively with respect to the will of God the Father (Matt 6:10; 7:21; 12:50; 18:14; 21:31; 26:42). If we look more broadly to the Synoptics as well as Acts, all except one speak of the will of God (Mk 3:35; Lk 12:47; 22:42; Acts 13:22; 21:14; 22:14; with Lk 23:25 referring to the will of the Jews).

Γίνομαι refers to something "coming into being or existence." Though very common and interpreted variously, it is important to note that γίνομαι portrays a distinct sense across all contexts, of something "*coming about.*" For example, when natural phenomena arrive (e.g. "and behold a great storm *arose* in the sea", Matt 8:24 c.f. 8:26; 27:45); when something comes into being (e.g. the birth of a child, Gal 4:4); when things come to pass (e.g., after the events of Jesus' arrest "all this *took place* to fulfil", Matt 25:56 c.f. 1:22); when a new epoch or time arrives (Matt 26:2); and when a person transitions to a particular state or mood (Matt 6:16).

The sense of the word is of a particular circumstance or event taking place, a new state of affairs coming about, or a noteworthy event occurring. This petition, then, is simply a request that the will of God the Father come about.[27]

---

disciples to remain ready for his coming which begin: "*Then* the kingdom of heaven will be like" (Matthew 25). This is not all that dissimilar to Christ's first appearing. Notice his confrontation with the Jews where he declares to them (in Matt 12:28) that the kingdom had "come upon them" even though they remained oblivious and rebellious. These events will take place regardless of people's readiness or prior activity. This indicates that the "coming" of the kingdom is God's activity, and not that of humanity in general, nor the church specifically.

[27] As has already been discussed, some commentators consider the first three petitions together as a prayer for the eschatological kingdom to be established. We will not repeat the arguments for that view here.

Obedience interpretation

Most scholars, however, suggest this is a prayer for the increase in obedience to God's law by human beings. Therefore, under the "obedience" interpretation, the third petition is granted when people obey, perhaps in increasing measure, the commands of Jesus.

Supporting this is the fact that Matthew often uses the noun θέλημα with respect to God's moral commands, as previously shown.[28] As a result, Nolland argues that: "Other uses of θέλημα ('will') in Matthew point us towards the same concern for obedience to God (Mt. 7:21; 12:50; 18:14; 21:31)… that in a comprehensive way people should come to act in conformity to the will of God."[29]

It is striking, however, that in all of the examples cited by Nolland, we find the verb ποιέω (meaning "to do") acting on θέλημα instead of γίνομαι as in Matthew 6:10. Davies and Allison are one of the few commentators to acknowledge this issue and suggest that "'Thy will be done' seems to be the passive formulation for ποιέω+θέλημα σου."[30] That is, since the verb ποιέω is rarely found in the passive voice at all, and never in the Synoptics, another verb is employed which is common in the passive voice.

Problems with the obedience interpretation

However, the obedience interpretation does not bear up to closer scrutiny for the following reasons. First, when θέλημα refers to the commandments of God, and obedience is commanded or described, ποιέω is used and not γίνομαι. There are six occasions where Matthew uses the noun θέλημα. Of these, three self-evidently refer to the moral commands of God which are to be carried out by people (7:21; 12:50; 21:31).[31] In each of these we find the verb ποιέω. The

---

[28] A key example, since it is also found in the Sermon on the Mount, is Matt 7:21: "Not everyone who says to me, 'Lord, Lord,' will enter the kingdom of heaven, but *the one who does the will* of my Father' (ὁ ποιῶν τὸ θέλημα τοῦ πατρός μου)." C.f. Matt 12:50; 21:31.

[29] Nolland, *Matthew*, 145–46.

[30] Davies & Allison, *Matthew*, 605–06.

[31] Note, Matt 18:14 does not deal directly with human obedience, but is instead a general statement of God's desire that all be saved.

same occurs without exception throughout the Synoptics and Acts (Mk 3:35; Lk 12:47; Acts 13:22).[32]

While Davies is correct that ποιέω does not appear in the passive voice, γίνομαι cannot be seen as an equivalent passive formulation. We have already defined γίνομαι as something "coming about". With respect to miracles and answered prayer it carries the sense of a new state of affairs coming to bear in the given context. Ποιέω, however, has to do with activity; that is, doing, making or producing something. Simply put, the words do not mean the same thing.[33]

Clearly the frequent rendering of γίνομαι (typically the aorist, passive, but sometimes the aorist middle) as "done" in English translations of the NT dilutes the distinction between it and ποιέω. C.A. Ries has undertaken an extensive study on the use of γίνομαι and its root γεν. He laments the loss of the real meaning and significance of γινομαι and says of the common translation "be done", "The Greek word (that) more nearly corresponding to our idea of doing is πράσσω to do, practice, effect exercise, be busy with, carry on, accomplish, perform. BE DONE does not convey the true idea of γίνομαι."[34]

His point is easily demonstrated. For example, in the English Standard Version γινομαι is translated "done" on nine occasions in Matthew. All refer to a miracle, prayer, or answer to prayer (6:10; 8:13; 9:29; 11:20, 21, 23; 15:28; 26:42). That is, when English translations use "done" to translate γινομαι, it is, in fact, the arrival of a new state of affairs, rather than human activity that is in view. On the other hand, when the ESV translates ποιέω as "done" it is always with respect to human activity (13:28; 23:23; 26:12, 13; 27:23). Here we see the understandable, but unfortunate, confusion from translating words with different definitions using the same

---

[32] Note Acts 22:14 speaks only of "knowing" God's will; Lk 23:25 speaks of the will of the Jews rather than God; Lk 22:42 and Acts 21:14 are quite similar to Matt 26:42 and will be dealt with below.

[33] We can observe this in the way γίνομαι is used throughout Matthew. The 75 references can be categorised into three groups: 24 have the sense of something "happening" (e.g. Matt 1:22); 38 have the sense of "becoming" such as a change of state (e.g. Matt 4:13); 13 are used in the context of miracles and prayer (e.g. Matt 8:13). None are associated with human behaviour or activity.

[34] C.A. Ries, "An Excursion with Ginomai" in *BETS* 5 No. 3 (1962), 69.

English word. They are not equivalent or interchangeable. C.A. Ries' detailed study into γίνομαι is illuminating.[35] He concludes: "These three essential factors lie inherent in this word γίνομαι: (1) It is a passive creative word. (2) Back of the creative act lies an intent, purpose, design. (3) It denotes *ingressive existence, a coming into being*: i.e., 'begin to be.'"[36]

Second, alongside this, the aorist imperative form of γίνομαι is exclusively used by Matthew in the context of answered prayer and miracles. There are five instances of this.[37] Three are used when Jesus is declaring a miracle into being. To the centurion: "let it *be done* for you as you have believed" (8:13); healing the blind: "according to your faith *be it done* to you" (9:29); healing a woman: "*be it done* for you as you desire" (15:28). The distinctive definition of γίνομαι can be clearly seen here. The healed state of affairs comes about at his word.

The remaining two, including the third petition, are prayers (6:10; 26:42).[38] We shall examine these further shortly. However, given what we have seen thus far, it is likely that a similar sense is intended. That is, the third petition is requesting that a miraculous state of affairs come about at God's command.[39]

The third problem with the obedience view is that it flattens out the concept of God's will to refer solely to the moral law of God that is able to be obeyed by humanity. However, God's will is regularly described in terms of God's sovereign activity and salvific purposes which may occur even *through* people's disobedience.

---

[35] There he laments "The loss of the real significance of the meaning of γίνομαι is most apparent." Ries, *BETS*, 68.

[36] Ries, *BETS*, 68.

[37] The imperative of γίνομαι is found eight times in Matthew as either aorist passive (6:10; 8:13; 9:29; 15:28; 26:42) or present middle/passive (6:16; 10:16; 24:44).[37] Incidentally, in each of the *present* imperatives a change in a person's state or mood is indicated. That is: "do not *become* gloomy" (6:16); "*be* wise" (10:16); and "*be* ready" (24:44). This is consistent with the middle voice.

[38] Note that five of the nine aorist passive imperatives are found in Matthew.

[39] Against this it could be argued that all six verbs in Matthew's version of the Lord's Prayer are aorist imperatives, and, in fact, most prayers take this form, therefore nothing should be made of it. However, Luke's version does contain a present imperative for the request for daily bread – indicating that it is a request for an ongoing day-by-day provision of food is in mind. This option was open to Matthew if that was his intention. Furthermore, the typical use of the aorist in NT prayers suggests that rather than diffusing the normal understanding of verbal forms, a one-time event is what is normally sought after.

This is seen throughout the NT. James, for example, speaks of this in his warning against boasting and presumption where he concludes: "Instead you ought to say, 'If the Lord wills (θέλω), we will live and do this or that'" (James 4:15). He is clearly not speaking of the moral law (since remaining alive is outside the human capacity to orchestrate!) but of God's sovereign will over all things. Another useful example is found in Acts 4 concerning the death of Christ. Despite the eager willingness of the perpetrators and that it was the most morally reprehensible of acts, the death of Jesus happened according to the prior planning of God (Acts 4:27–28).

We also see the noun θέλημα used of the will of God in a non-moral sense in Matthew 18:14: "It is not the will of my Father who is in heaven that one of these little ones should perish." This is not a command that people can obey, which demonstrates that the will of God is more complex.

Therefore, while the NT often speaks of God's will in moral terms which people can obey, it also speaks of God's sovereign will where his broader purposes are served. If this level of God's will is applied to the third petition, it takes on a completely different meaning. It is, in fact, the more likely interpretation.

With doubts about the obedience interpretation in mind, and by paying close attention to the definition and usage of the relevant words, another approach now presents itself. That is, the third petition is *a prayer for God to bring about his sovereign purposes.*

The Third Petition in the NT

This is also the most natural reading of the three other instances where γινομαι and θελημα form a similar construction as in Matthew 6:10: Matthew 26:42, Luke 22:42, and Acts 21:14. These are undoubtedly the most useful guide in understanding the third petition.

Matthew 26:42 and Luke 22:42 are their respective accounts of the prayer that Jesus uttered in Gethsemane. Matthew records: "My Father, if this cannot pass unless I drink it, your will be done" (γενηθήτω τὸ θέλημά σου, the exact same construction as in 6:10). Jesus is awaiting his arrest and certain death with full knowledge of what was to come. Some commentators who take the obedience view assume that Jesus is praying for his own obedience. But that is surely ignoring the context. The circumstances were upon Jesus, and the thrust of the prayer was one of submissive obedience in allowing the circumstances in train to unfold as God had ordained.

Luke records: "Nevertheless, not my will, but yours, be done" (πλὴν μὴ τὸ θέλημά μου ἀλλὰ τὸ σὸν γινέσθω). Luke uses γινομαι in the present tense, which he is more prone to do, but there is no material difference in meaning.

Interestingly, in both accounts Jesus tells the disciples to pray that they do not "enter into temptation" lest they fall into sin through fear. This is surely harking back to the sixth petition of the Lord's Prayer. Jesus himself does not utter that prayer which suggests falling into personal sin was not his primary concern. Rather it was the impending circumstances that would result in his death that prompted the prayer of trust and submission to the sovereign purposes of the Father.

Finally, in Acts 21 Paul's companions were urging him not to go to Jerusalem because a prophet had warned him of the persecution that awaited him there. Luke records: "And since he would not be persuaded, we ceased and said, 'Let the will of the Lord be done'" (Τοῦ κυρίου τὸ θέλημα γινέσθω). Paul felt called to visit Jerusalem despite the danger. Clearly it is not a matter of sin or obedience to the moral law here. Instead, it appears his companions are praying a prayer of trust that God's intended circumstances would come about in the face of potential suffering.

This, it seems, is the best way to interpret the third petition.[40] The usage of this prayer in the NT aligns well with our earlier finding concerning the definition of γίνομαι. It is significant that the context was one of suffering which lay ahead for both Jesus and Paul in their specific callings. It is particularly in this context that the prayer takes on this unique and rich application.[41] Finally, it seems unlikely that this third petition is an explanation of the second, or that they are synonymous.

---

[40] We do not have space to deal exhaustively with the added phrase "as in heaven, also upon the earth" here. Most commentators agree that a contrast is being made. Also, whether this phrase applies to all three petitions or just the third does not affect the findings we have made thus far.

[41] See also *TDNT*, 55.

Conclusion

We conclude, therefore, that the second petition is a prayer for the eschatological ushering in of the kingdom. It is not a request for the gradual coming of the kingdom in some sense. The third petition is not specifically a prayer for the increase in obedience. Instead it asks that God's sovereign purposes come about. It is a prayer of trust and submission to God's unfolding plan in the circumstances that lie ahead. It appears that Jesus offered it as a model prayer without reference to any particular situation. This is made clear by the two examples that exist in the NT where both Jesus and Paul prayed this prayer in the face of suffering. For each, their respective callings required them to walk through difficult circumstances and uncertain times. In such occasions, it is appropriate to pray in submission and trust "your will be done."

Facing Polemics Head On: Learning Christology "From the Side"

Christoph Ochs

Worldview Centre for Intercultural Studies

Introduction

When it comes to doing theology today — and Christology in particular — we find that "what is true is seldom new, what is new is seldom true."[1] But, there was a time when this witticism did not apply, when Christology was not fully articulated, not thought through. In fact, the early church had to face constant and potent theological challenges from within and without. And these challenges were faced head on.

Today we have the privilege of being able to fall back on the great ecumenical creeds of the fourth and fifth century and their miscellanea. Likewise, we have the advantage of having clearly defined, highly sophisticated critical editions of the New Testament at our fingertips. The Christian communities of the second century, for example, still had to wrangle over the nature and extent of the canon — a struggle which we hardly have to face today.[2] In that sense we have clear advantages, we have creed and canon, deposits of truth that come with extensive commentaries ancient and new. We do not have to reinvent the wheel, and we *must not* if we want to stay within the trajectory of orthodox Christianity.

---

[1] Based on a German proverb: "*Das Wahre ist selten neu, das Neue selten wahr,*" which perhaps is based on a couplet by Johan Heinrich Voss: "Dein redseliges Buch lehrt mancherlei Neues und Wahres, wäre das Wahre nur neu, und das Neue nur Wahr!" (Vossischer Musenalmanach 1792). See Wolfgang Jacobmeyer, *Das Deutsche Schulgeschichtsbuch 1700–1945: Die erste Epoche seiner Gattungsgeschichte im Spiegel der Vorworte, Band 1* (Geschichtskultur und Historisches Lernen 8; Berlin: Lit, 2011), 609, n. 259.

[2] Nowadays, the discovery of "lost" or "secret" versions of the gospels cannot become a significant challenge to the canon of Scripture; they and any future discoveries can safely be dismissed precisely because there was no Christian faith community who retained and "traditioned" them as *Scripture*. This point has been explored by Roland Deines, "The Term and Concept of Scripture," in *What Is Bible?* (eds. Armin Lange and Karin Finsterbusch; Leuven: Peeters, 2012), 235–81 (see 274–75), and idem, "Revelatory Experiences as the Beginning of Scripture: Paul's Letters and the Prophets in the Hebrew Bible," in *From Author to Copyist: Essays on the Composition, Redaction, and Transmission of the Hebrew Bible in the Honor of Zipi Talshir* (ed. Cana Werman; Winona Lake, Indiana: Eisenbrauns, 2015), 303–36 (see 317–19, 322–23).

However, the danger for those who want to do Christology today is to *not* squarely face the challenges because of having such a repository of answers. "Christology for a New Generation" of course cannot be so innovative in its fresh articulation that it forgets the hard learned lessons from the past.[3] But, the disadvantage that comes with having creed and canon is often a lack of awareness of the weight of the objections; to never have really heard the voices coming "from the side."[4] Especially when it comes to Christology it was the voices coming from the outside, from the periphery, often from the majority, that created an existential need for theological reflection and response. And quite often these outside voices were also inside voices.[5]

In this paper I hope to show briefly why it is needful for any new generation to listen carefully to challenges coming "from the side," challenges that have been persistent and are potent, to learn that theology benefits from this exercise, and to perhaps discover that these challenges (and responses) are not so new after all. This is how the church has done theology, and this pattern we should follow. In that respect, it is like a mother's caution to "listen before you speak."

---

[3] The conference theme was "Jesus Christ — For Us Today: Christology for a New Generation," Paradosis Conference, 15 August 2016, Melbourne School of Theology. The call for papers included the following text: "Christians have been discussing the person of Jesus Christ for more than 2000 years. Yet over the centuries the discussion has lost nothing of its relevance and appeal. While we honour those who have gone before us, we are convinced that every generation ought to articulate afresh its faith in the person and work of Jesus Christ."

[4] I take the idea of Christology "from the side," rather than from "above" or "below" from Bruce J. Malina and Jerome H. Neyrey, *Calling Jesus Names: The Social Value of Labels in Matthew* (Sonoma, Cal.: Polebridge, 1988). This term was also appropriated by Scot McKnight and Joseph B. Modica, eds., *Who Do My Opponents Say That I Am? An Investigation of the Accusations Against the Historical Jesus* (LNTS 358; London: T&T Clark, 2008). Malina and Neyrey contend that "within Christian groups before Constantine, the chief expressive social dimension for non-Roman and Roman non-elite Christians was not vertical, but horizontal — 'from the side.' This is the human perspective and social arrangement marked by the relational inside and outside, center and periphery... [O]ur task will be to describe Christology as it was articulated from the outside and from the inside, that is, how Jesus was evaluated by his enemies and his followers. This is Christology 'from the side'" (op. cit., x). I question if the Christology on the horizontal plane, specifically "on the inside," would have been articulated by the insiders much differently from the so-called Christology "from above/below," especially when we attest an early high Christology. Nevertheless, I find the idea of Christology "from the side" a helpful one.

[5] Walter Bauer has shown that the demarcation between what is "in" (orthodoxy) and what is "out" (heterodoxy) was far from clear in the early centuries of the church; see Walter Bauer, *Orthodoxy and Heresy in Earliest Christianity* (London: SCM Press, 1972).

The Constant Challenge of Christ[6]

From the very beginning of the Christian story, the message about Christ has been scandalous (cf. 1 Cor 1:23). From within and without the faith community objections to the proclamation that *this* Jesus is the Son of God incarnate — even "God with us" (Matt 1:23) — have been persistent and articulate.[7] Historically, Christians have listened to these challenges coming "from the side" and it is precisely this which lies behind the articulation of theology and the great creeds.

Because the belief in the full divinity of Jesus has been challenged at all times, it is therefore false to think that it was merely the naiveté of earlier "pre-critical" generations that allowed such a high view of Jesus to prevail unchallenged. It was challenged, constantly, over centuries, by formidable thinkers from within and without the Christian community. For that reason alone it is worthwhile investigating those challenges.

Nevertheless, the authors of the New Testament, the church apologists, and theologians before and during the Middle Ages maintained the paradox of Christology as a *necessary element in the description of the "real" Jesus*, when it would have been much easier to abandon the embarrassments of the incarnation and humiliation of Christ. Contemporary taboos, some of which persist to this day, and strongly held metaphysical beliefs should have stifled, if not stopped, a Christology that embraced and proclaimed the full humanity and full deity of Jesus Christ.

And, as any student of early church history comes to know, this struggle over the understanding of Christ and of God was not just a struggle with external voices. The so called Arian controversy, for example, was a controversy precisely because Arian Christology was not only a popular, but also a plausible way of explaining

---

[6] The points I am making in this paragraph are taken from the introduction of my dissertation, *Matthaeus Adversus Christianos: The Use of the Gospel of Matthew in Jewish Polemics Against the Divinity of Jesus* (WUNT II/350; Tübingen: Mohr Siebeck, 2013), 1–6.

[7] Although it is not the incarnation *per se* that is the *scandalon*, rather as Bonhoeffer writes: "The offence caused by Jesus Christ is not his incarnation — that indeed is revelation — but his humiliation. The humanity of Christ and his humiliation should be carefully distinguished," Dietrich Bonhoeffer, *Christology* (trans. John Bowden; London: Collins, 1966), 46–47.

Christ.[8] At a time when christological orthodoxy was not fully articulated, the Arian model was actually viable, and perhaps even preferable, because it avoided certain metaphysical embarrassments. Of course, one of the reason why that did not happen is because the church did carefully consider these voices "from the side." In the case of the Arian controversy, Athanasius pointed out that this christological explanation redefined and undermined the established understanding of salvation.[9]

Another prime example of listening to the side would be Irenaeus' detailed, mind-numbing examination of various gnostic beliefs, teasing out possible inherent contradictions or clashes with established doctrine in his *Against Heresies*. In fact, the existence of the entire *Adversus haereses* and *Adversus judaeos* genre with its many examples demonstrates that the early church intently listened — and had to listen — to alternate truth claims, though it must be said some protagonists heard better than others.[10]

And so it is the constant challenge of Christ, the voices that object and question, which really become the midwives of theology. In other words, it is the vitality and potency of another truth claim that brings about the creation of responses and theological reflection.

Listening to the Voices from the Side

So, Christians have listened to challenges coming "from the side." In fact, it is this that had decisive and positive impact on the articulation of Christology, so much so that without knowing the challenges it becomes difficult to fully understand the creeds.

---

[8] For the rationale behind Arian thinking see, e.g., Richard P. C. Hanson, *The Search for the Christian Doctrine of God: The Arian Controversy 318–381* (Edinburgh: T&T Clark, 1988), 99–122.

[9] According to Athanasius' famous dictum, "for he became man, so that we might become god" (Αὐτὸς γὰρ ἐνηνθρώπησεν, ἵνα ἡμεῖς θεωποιηθῶμεν), *Inc.* 54.3 (PG 25:192B), salvation was understood as *theosis*. Athanasius' Christology won the day *because it aligned with the established understanding of soteriology* (see, e.g., Jn 14:20; Rom 8:17; 2 Pet 1:4; Clement, *Protr.* 1; Justin, *Dial.* 124; Irenaeus, *Haer.* 4.38.4), which consequently mandated a union of the divine and the human in Christ. Christ had to be fully divine in order to offer participation in the divine nature. The christological paradox was embraced because it corresponded with the church's tradition and experience of salvation. For a shorter introduction see Stephen Finlan and Vladimir Kharlamov (eds.), *Theosis: Deification in Christian Theology* (Vol. 1; Cambridge, UK: James Clarke, 2006), esp. the essay by Jeffrey Finch, "Athanasius on the Deifying Work of the Redeemer," 104–121.

[10] Irenaeus seems to have listened carefully as a comparison with Nag Hammadi texts shows; for a short discussion see Matthew C. Steenberg, *Irenaeus on Creation: The Cosmic Christ and the Saga of Redemption* (VCSup 91; Leiden: Brill, 2008), 11–15.

When one carefully listens to the polemics, the objections, and even allows these to stir up doubts, only then will one come to understand the questions and the existential pressure behind them that drove the articulation of theology. The creeds and christological statements, the controversies, they are really the responses to these questions. But, if we do not allow ourselves to feel the weight of these questions, then the creeds and theology remain stale and irrelevant to our current contexts. It is unfortunate that the authorities often have attempted to purge these voices and writings in the aftermath, so that we often have to piece together what the actual objections were.[11]

And, I would argue that teaching theology from the creeds without *first* challenging students with the questions *and* allowing them to struggle with those questions, is one of the things that makes theological study often feel irrelevant. Knowing and understanding the question is often more important than knowing the answer.

Now, listening does not mean hearing the argument and then to immediately return with a response or answer. This is a temptation and it often leads to a parody of the original objection. Listening means to take the objection seriously and to allow the alternative truth claim, the alternate explanation that is offered to inform one's own thinking. At the very least, it gives insight in the objectors' way of thinking. This requires a certain openness to new ideas, courage, and patience. It is this willingness to listen and explore that brings about a fuller articulation and understanding of orthodoxy. In other words, we do not have to fear or shun the voices "from the side," we ought to welcome them.

Let me give several examples to illustrate why it is worthwhile and illuminating to listen to the voices "from the side." One of the first

---

[11] Prime examples would be Celsus' *Logos Alethes*, Porphyry's *Adversus Christianos*, or the various writings of Arian bishops, including Arius' *Thalia*. Some of the arguments have been reconstructed, see, e.g., Robert Louis Wilken, *The Christians as the Romans Saw Them* (New Haven: Yale University Press, 1984, 2003); John G. Cook, *The Interpretation of the New Testament in Greco-Roman Paganism* (STAC 3; Tübingen: Mohr Siebeck, 2000; repr. Peabody: Hendrickson, 2002); Celsus, *On the True Doctrine: A Discourse Against the Christians* (trans. R. Joseph Hoffmann; Oxford: Oxford University Press, 1987); Robert M. Berchman, *Porphyry Against the Christians* (Ancient Mediterranean and Medieval Texts and Contexts 1; Leiden: Brill 2005). For Jewish objections see Daniel J. Lasker, *Jewish Philosophical Polemics against Christianity in the Middle Ages* (2nd ed.; Oxford: The Littman Library of Jewish Civilization, 2007), or my *Matthaeus Adversus Christianos*.

of these voices was Marcion.[12] Now, Marcion was actually an insider and the heterodox ideas he voiced (or amplified) are surprisingly resilient, as we will see. Of course we only can call them heterodox because he in effect helped the church to find her orthodoxy. Because of that his voice is somewhat muffled and largely lives on only in the writings of those who responded to him, in this case Tertullian:

Marcion — Gentile Christian heterodox leader (c. 85–160 AD)

> Beginning then with that nativity you [Marcion] so strongly object to, orate, attack now, the nastiness of genital elements in the womb, the filthy curdling of moisture and blood, and of the flesh to be for nine months nourished on that same mire. Draw a picture of the womb getting daily more unmanageable, heavy, self-concerned, safe not even in sleep, uncertain in the whims of dislikes and appetites… You shudder, of course, at the child passed out along with the afterbirth, and of course bedaubed with it.[13]

According to Tertullian, Marcion rejected the full incarnation of Christ because of the associated taboos of a mammalian birth; to think of Christ born of a woman. Perish the thought! This may perhaps also be the reason for the omission of the nativity accounts in Marcion's bible version.[14] If so, a good case can be made that it is Marcion's high view of god that acts as his motivation, for it is unbecoming to associate this good and pure god and savior with the facts of human life and any all too anthropomorphic depictions.[15] It

---

[12] For a recent attempt of recovering the "historical Marcion" see Judith M. Lieu, *Marcion and the Making of a Heretic: God and Scripture in the Second Century* (Cambridge: Cambridge University Press, 2015).

[13] Tertullian, *De Carne Christi* 4. Translated by Ernest Evans, *Tertullians's Treatise on the Incarnation* (London: SPCK, 1956), 13. It is not clear if this is in fact Marcion's polemic or something that Tertullian puts in his mouth; regardless, it is a potent challenge.

[14] Marcion of Sinope/Pontus is commonly known as having created for himself and his church a more suitable bible with some significant omissions (akin to Thomas Jefferson), although it must be said that much of what is known about him comes from his opponents' writings. It is, therefore, not entirely clear if and what Marcion precisely cut out from his gospel edition, in particular since it is presumably related to an early version of the gospel of Luke, see Lieu, *Marcion*, 367–73, and Dieter Roth, *The Text of Marcion's Gospel* (NTTS 49; Leiden: Brill, 2015), 1–45.

[15] I would tentatively suggest that it is this aspect of Marcion's theology that is detrimental to his asceticism, his views of human sexuality, the incarnation, and of the god of the Hebrew Bible as a lesser god. Lieu reminds us that "Marcion could not have made the impact he undoubtedly did if his questions and his answers had not resonated among his hearers; neither would he have made that impact if he had had nothing more to offer than did many others" (op. cit., p. 11). Tertullian quotes Marcion as saying: "'But,' you [Marcion] say, 'the reason why I deny that God was really and truly changed into man, in the sense of being both

would seem Marcion had listened to the voices "from the side," and *agreeing with them*, his solution was to cut out the humiliating aspects of the incarnation.[16] His intention would have been honorable and reasonable, for he sought to remove Christ from the kind of taboo polemics we hear repeated by pagan philosophers, such as Celsus and Porphyry:

Celsus — Platonist philosopher (c. 180 AD)
> And if he [= God] did wish to send down a spirit from himself, why did he have to breathe it into the womb of a woman? He already knew how to make men. He could have formed a body for this one also without having to thrust his own spirit into such foul pollution.[17]

Porphyry — Neo-Platonist philosopher (c. 234–305 AD)
> But if anyone among the Greeks were so frivolous that he would assume that the gods live in these statues, his idea would be a much purer one than those who believe that the deity came down into the womb of the Virgin Mary and became an embryo. And then when he was born he was placed in swaddling clothes. For this is a place full of blood and gall and things even more disgusting than these.[18]

It is easy to underestimate the potency of this kind of argument, to perhaps just think of it as an antiquated kind of sexism or a cheap polemic. No doubt, the taboo aspect of the idea of god being born and its graphic nature made it a readily understood challenge. This argument could be heard in the streets and alleys. This is how you pummel your Christian neighbour.[19] But the real challenge of this

---

born and corporated in flesh [sic; *et carne corporaretur*], is that he who is without end must of necessity also be unchangeable: for to be changed into something else is an ending of what originally was: therefore change is inapplicable to one to whom ending is inapplicable,'" Tertullian, *De Carne Christi* 3 (Evans, 11). Marcion's metaphysics, in particular the emphasis of the transcendence of god, would seem to inform his theological commitments. The fact that Marcionism was so vehemently opposed by the early church demonstrates that this must have resonated with a significant number of Christians.

[16] Other heterodox forms of Christian belief, e.g., (so-called) Docetism, Arianism, and Apollinarianism all seek to avoid associating the divine with any notion of passability, though their solutions of course differ significantly. Nevertheless, this goes to show how strong these voices from the side really were, and how these voices were not just in the periphery but were much at the centre of theological articulation.

[17] Origen, *Contra Celsum* 6.73. Translated by Henry Chadwick, *Origen: Contra Celsum* (Cambridge: Cambridge University Press, 1965), 386.

[18] Translated by Robert M. Berchman, *Porphyry Against the Christians* (Leiden: Brill, 2005), §208, 217; cf. Macarius Magnes, *Apokritikos* 4.22.

[19] A comparable example is the so called *Alexamenos graffito*, a second century anti-Christian drawing of a crucifixion scene with a donkey headed Christ inscribed with the line "Alexamenos worships God." For a detailed discussion see Oliver L. Yarbrough, "The

idea lies in the largely shared, common concept of God. Greeks and Jews essentially had an equally high view of the transcendence of God and held to a strict divine/human, creator/creation dichotomy.[20] And this is, of course, one of the reasons it took centuries to articulate and agree on the mystery of the nature of Christ. But, this is also why these voices, these arguments, do not go away. We hear it echo through the centuries:

Anonymous Jewish writer — Near East (c. 6–9th century AD)

It is most astonishing, how is it that you, who claim to be judicious and reasonable, are not ashamed: ashamed of yourself and embarrassed by me; [ashamed] that you worship a god who dwelt in the womb, in the filth of menstrual blood, in the confinement and imprisonment and darkness for nine months; he lay in a donkey's manger and he was nursed at the breast of a harlot.[21]

Joseph Qimḥi — Medieval rabbi, France/Spain (c. 1105?–1170? AD)

The great and mighty God Whom no eye has seen, Who has neither form nor image, Who said 'For man may not see Me and live (Exod. 33:20) — how shall I believe that this great inaccessible *Deus absconditus* needlessly entered the womb of a woman, the filthy, foul bowels of a female, compelling the living God to be born of a woman, a child without knowledge or understanding, senseless, unable to distinguish between his right hand and his left, defecating and urinating, sucking his mother's breasts from hunger and thirst, crying when he is thirsty so that his mother will have compassion on him. Indeed, if she had not suckled him, he would have died of hunger like other people. If not, why should she have suckled him? He should have lived miraculously! Why should she have suckled him for nothing, that he should engage in all foul and miserable human

---

Shadow of an Ass: On Reading the Alexamenos Graffito," in *Text, Image, and Christians in the Graeco-Roman World: A Festschrift in Honor of David Lee Balch* (eds. Aliou Cissé Niang and Carolyn Osiek; PTMS 176; Eugene, Or.: Pickwick, 2012), 239–54.

[20] How strict this dichotomy was during the Second Temple period is a matter of very recent debate, see e.g., Daniel Boyarin's or Crispin Fletcher-Louis' work. But it is fair to say that with the rise and influence of Christianity this dichotomy became more pronounced, so that eventually only Christians could hold to a duality or mixture of natures, whereas Jews and Muslims denied the mere possibility. But even within Christian thinking, there always was the temptation to over-emphasize one aspect, whether it be the divinity of Christ (Docetism, Sabellianism, Apollinarianism, etc.) or his humanity (Ebionism, Arianism, etc.).

[21] Daniel J. Lasker, and Sarah Stroumsa (eds.), *The Polemic of Nestor the Priest: Introduction: Annotated Translations and Commentary* (2 vols.; Jerusalem: Ben-Zvi Institute for the Study of Jewish Communities in the East, 1996), vol. 1, 68 (§82). The latter refers to Salome (not Mary), who according to the apocryphal sources, *The Proto-Evangelium of James*, *The History of Joseph the Carpenter*, and *The Infancy Gospel of Pseudo-Matthew*, was Jesus' wet-nurse and Mary's midwife.

practices? Thus I do not profess this belief which you profess, for my reason does not allow me to diminish the greatness of God, be He exalted, for He has not lessened His glory, be He exalted, nor has He reduced His splendor, be He extolled. If I do not profess this faith which you profess, I am not blameworthy. I say to you further that if this belief is true, the Creator would not hold me guilty for not believing in His deficiency and the reduction of His grandeur and splendor… I do not in this respect believe in the diminution of His glory and greatness… I may liken this for you to a human king who changed his garments, shaved his hair, and put on filthy garb and dirty clothes, so that he impaired his noble figure. He then walked alone on the highways without dignity or majesty. The people came and told someone: 'This is the king.' If he does not believe [it], the king cannot hold it against him. How much more evident is this with respect to the King of kings, the Holy One, blessed be He. Who would dare to profess this belief which diminishes His greatness, whereby He cannot save His world except by humiliating Himself, debasing His majesty, and befouling His splendor.[22]

International Islamic Federation of Student Organizations (1985)

Reason refuses to accept a man who was born of a woman, suffered from human wants, ignorance and limitations, and gradually grew in stature, power and wisdom like all other human beings, as God. To put human limitations upon God and to believe in His incarnation in a human body is to deny the perfection of God.[23]

Of course the church has responded to these voices. The hypostatic union, in a way, is an answer; and others have been given.[24] But the

---

[22] Joseph Kimḥi, *The Book of the Covenant* (trans. by Frank Talmage; Mediaeval Sources in Translation 12; Toronto: Pontifical Institute of Mediaeval Studies, 1972), 36–37.

[23] Ulfat Asiz-us-Samad, *Islam and Christianity* (Safat, Kuwait: Sahaba Islamic Press, 1985), 38.

[24] E.g., Odo of Tournai (c. 1060–1113) responded to a very similar argument. A Jewish dialogue partner, Leo, tells Odo: "In one thing especially we laugh at you and think that you are crazy. You say that God was conceived within his mother's womb, surrounded by vile fluid, and suffered enclosure within this foul prison for nine months when finally, in the tenth month, he emerged from her private parts (who is not embarrassed by such a scene!). This you attribute to God what is most unbecoming, which we would not do without great embarrassment," Irvin M. Resnick, *On Original Sin and a Disputation with the Jew, Leo, Concerning the Advent of Christ, the Son of God: Theological Treatises, Odo of Tournai* (Philadelphia: University of Pennsylvania Press, 1994), 95. Odo's answer follows: "God fills all things and is everywhere whole. Although he fills us and is whole even in us who are sinners, he is untouched by the uncleanness of our sins, but remains uncontaminated and pure. He sees all things and nothing hurts him. He sees darkness yet remains untouched by the darkness, since 'light shines in darkness' (Jn. 1:5) and 'night, just like day will be illuminated' (Ps. 138:12 Vulg.). The Most Pure sees sin, and the Most Just sees our injustices, since he justly orders every evil he sees. The light of justice is not extinguished by making sins visible, just as the

point I wish to stress here is that Christology for a new generation does well to intently listen to these kind of voices "from the side," for it is there that Christology begins, it is there where it is articulated, learnt, and tested.[25]

Learning Christology from the Side

Having listened to some of the voices from the side, how do we learn then? As already said, by listening intently, and patiently, by seeking to understand what these voices say, the church was alerted to real issues, as well as misunderstandings.[26] We likewise, if we listen, should be alerted to real issues and misunderstandings — including our own, as we should hopefully become more aware of our own subjectivisms, biases, and place in history. This is where Christology for a new generation ought to begin. By doing so, we, like the church before us, have to come to explore, reject, or endorse various alternate ideas about Christ and God; the end product being such doctrines as the Trinity or the hypostatic union. Today we hold these as the bedrock of Christian orthodoxy, and we can think about trinitarian "this or that," something unthinkable in the second century. We learned these things because we listened, and because of it we were enriched, and our understanding grew.

Of course, the fact that certain voices and objections remain with us to this day unchanged, as we just noticed, is because they touch upon a central mystery and paradox. Christology is and will ever remain inherently mysterious because here the finite and infinite meet. To quote Augustine, "if you understand it, it is not God" (*si enim comprehendis non est deus*).[27] In other words, we should expect it to be complicated if we affirm that God is incarnational and Christ somehow is divine.

It should then not be a surprise that listening to these voices from the side has a direct impact on the two major ways of doing

---

light of this world shines upon the sordid fleshly body but is not soiled by it. Why then are you offended if God is conceived in a virgin, when he preserves his purity everywhere?" (op. cit.).

[25] It is equally important to realize that the inner Christian debates are not just motivated by philosophical considerations and politics (which they were), but especially by polemics. There were powerful outside voices that shaped the conversation.

[26] This is perhaps analogous to the primacy of thoughtful observation (*Sehakt*) in Adolf Schlatter's theology, see Michael Bräutigam, *Union with Christ: Adolf Schlatter's Relational Christology* (Eugene, Or.: Pickwick, 2015), 107–110.

[27] Augustine of Hippo, *Sermo* 117.3.5.

theology. One is the negative (the *via negativa*, the apophatic) and one is the positive (the cataphatic).

When we think of the negative, by listening the church learned to articulate what Christology was not; e.g., the hypostatic union was defined by the negative adverbs *inconfuse, immutabiliter, indivise,* and *inseparabiliter*.[28] In that sense, theological articulation is often reactionary and apophatic, and that is inherent to the subject matter. It is okay to be reactionary and negative. In other words, after having listened thoughtfully, when it comes to articulating Christology, there is nothing wrong about rejecting certain voices. These voices, in fact, become the parameters that narrow down the area in which we can do Christology. By listening carefully, we can learn what we do not believe, and why.

Positively, we can see that the questions and voices from the side maneuver us to articulate and endorse theological insights. For example, rather than relegating the incarnation to a footnote of history, it was embraced and became central to the understanding of the work and nature of God. Or in the words of Gregory of Nazianzus: "What is not assumed has not been healed, but that which has been united to his Godhead is also saved."[29] In other words, we can be grateful to Arianism that it helped us fully embrace the grandeur of the incarnation, that it helped us to see even more clearly that salvation means to be truly united to Christ. This then is one of the big benefits of listening to the voices "from the side." Like midwives (though perhaps unwillingly), they lead us through the process of better articulating the great acts of God — "birthing theology" as it were.[30] There are of course also minor benefits to listening to these voices, e.g., medieval Jewish polemicists anticipated the quest for the historical Jesus by some

---

[28] Or rather, ἀσυγχύτως, ἀτρέπτως, ἀδιαιρέτως, and ἀχωρίστως, negative qualifiers which are a concession to the inability to coherently describe the "'how' of the divine and the human existence coexisted in the same person," Vladimir Lossky, "Christological Dogma," in *Orthodox Theology: An Introduction* (trans. Ian and Ihita Kesarcodi-Watson; Crestwood, N.Y.: St Vladimir's Seminary Press, 1978), 95–118, here 99.

[29] Gregory of Nazianzus, *Ep.* 101, 32 (SC 208, 50).

[30] This notion, namely, that the church progressively articulated already held theological beliefs, rather than "invented" them, and that this process is triggered by certain events (or voices) is explored in much greater depth by Anthony C. Thiselton, *The Hermeneutics of Doctrine* (Grand Rapids: Eerdmans, 2007). By means of this process dispositions become positions.

500 years.[31] In other words, there is much to gain and learn from listening to the voices "from the side."

The moral of the story, then, is to listen carefully, to face the voices "from the side." That is how theology was done in the past, and that is how theological thinking has advanced. Whoever wants to do Christology for a new generation first should have to listen to the voices of that generation. If they are the same voices than those of the past, then the insights of the early church can be brought to the table; if they are new, then the exciting quest of articulating fresh theological insights can begin. In either case, theology should be done only after listening.

---

[31] Unfortunately, because Christians did not listen to their Jewish counterparts, this was a missed opportunity. See Ochs, *Matthaeus Adversus Christianos*, 266–67.

The Kenotic Christology of P. T. Forsyth

Bradley M. Penner

Prairie College & Briercrest Seminary, Canada

Introduction

The person and work of Jesus Christ is the most important doctrine in the entirety of the Christian faith, and as such every aspect of his personhood and ministry must be scrutinized and delineated to appreciate and comprehend the utter magnitude of God becoming flesh in Jesus of Nazareth. The soteriological ramifications that stem from the necessity of properly understanding who Jesus was and what his contemporary relevance is are immense considering the assertion that if one does not know who Jesus is, then his salvific benefits are of no consequence. Therefore, it is even more imperative that a holistic approach is taken in explicating the person and work of Jesus Christ in order that God may be glorified as lord and saviour of humanity.

One of the most difficult and controversial aspects of the doctrine of Jesus Christ is that of the *kenosis*. Traditionally, the church and her theologians have understood this divine divesting as a simple "veiling" (*krypsis*), but since the nineteenth century certain theologians have argued that, in assuming human flesh, the pre-existent Christ set aside certain (or all) attributes and thereby "emptied himself" of not only his divine prerogatives but also of his *divine nature*. This interpretive tradition became known as *kenotic Christology* because of its emphasis on the argument that the Son of God literally "emptied himself" of certain (or all) of his divine attributes in the incarnation of Christ. This tradition's two chief proponents are Gottfried Thomasius (1802–1875) and P.T. Forsyth (1848–1921) who, although having different theological emphases, contend that the *kenosis* is not a veiling (*krypsis*) of the deity and divine attributes, but an actual "emptying" (*kenosis*) of it.

In this essay, it shall be argued that the kenotic Christology of P.T. Forsyth is founded upon the premise that the *kenosis* began in the pre-existence of Christ, that in the incarnation the *kenosis* was a moral act of God with the concentration of the divine attributes from a state of actuality to potentiality, and that the *kenosis* was completed by a necessary *plerosis*, which was accomplished in the moral conquest of Christ.

Kenotic Theology

To better understand the importance of Forsyth's contribution to theology in general and Christology in particular, one must first become cognizant of the tradition and hermeneutical trajectory that preceded and influenced him known as *kenotic theology*. "Kenotic theology is a theology that focuses on the person of Christ in terms of some form of self-limitation by the pre-existent Son in his becoming man. Kenotic theology at the theoretical level is a way of conceiving of the incarnation that is relatively new in the history of reflection on the person of Christ."[1]

The chief, paradigmatic passage of Scripture that kenotic theologians emphasize is that of the christological hymn of Philippians 2:6–11, especially verse 7. Whereas some translations translate *kenosis* idiomatically as referring to Christ having "made himself nothing" (NIV and ESV) or "made himself of no reputation" (KJV and NKJV), others prefer to translate *kenosis* more literally as "emptied himself" (RSV and NASB). Therefore, it is no surprise that "there has been much discussion about this entire crucial passage (2:6–11), and several interpretations exist today."[2] Of these several interpretations it is also important to note that "some see this form of thought about Christ as the most recent advance in Christology; others see it as a blind alley."[3]

Kenotic theology, however, is not as new as some may perceive, for in the patristic era the *kenosis* of Christ was utilized in the many christological and trinitarian controversies. In the famous debates between Athanasius and Arius, Cyril and Nestorius, and Leo and Eutyches the *kenosis* showed "the divine decision that the Word should become man [indicating] a genuine humbling. For God, the Incarnation is not an 'increase' but an emptying, an exhaustion."[4]

However, as the debates raged over the hypostatic union of the two natures of Christ and how God could assume flesh and yet remain immutable in his essence, the *kenosis* remained a relatively mute doctrine because of its challenge to the entrenched philosophical

---

[1] S.M. Smith, "Kenosis, Kenotic Theology," in *Evangelical Dictionary of Theology*, ed. Walter Elwell (Grand Rapids: Baker, 2001), 651.

[2] Smith, 651.

[3] Smith, 651.

[4] Emilio Brito, "Kenosis," in *Encyclopedia of Christian Theology*, ed. Jean-Yves Lacoste (New York: Routledge, 2005), 2:853.

and metaphysical presuppositions held by many theologians in the patristic era.

Although kenotic theology lay dormant for centuries because of the prevailing Hellenistic metaphysics in theology, a slight resurgence manifested during the Protestant Reformation period. Along with the many lost and distorted doctrines that were retrieved and reformulated by Martin Luther, his reviving of the *Communicatio Idiomatum* aided in the renaissance of the *kenosis*. "According to [Luther], certain attributes of the divine nature of Christ become attributes of human nature."[5] This led certain Lutheran theologians, such as Martin Chemnitz, to argue that "Christ possessed divine majesty in his humanity and during his earthly life but customarily refrained from using it. It was only upon his glorification that he would make use of it."[6]

Nevertheless, Greek metaphysical categories still reigned in Western Christian theology until the Post-Reformation era, when the first formal kenotic Christologies began to be formulated and delineated in response to the numerous aporias regarding Chalcedonian Christology.

> The kenoticists shared the new dissatisfaction with the aporias of classical formulations, but they were, for the most part, still committed to the spirit and intentions of the creeds. They attempted to mediate between the legitimate new emphasis on the humanity of Jesus and what they held to be the legitimate intuitions of traditional Christology.[7]

Therefore, kenotic theology is not an entirely new doctrine, but one that is rooted in canonical Scripture, utilized in apologetics, and seminal for a more holistic christological reflection and confession.

Gottfried Thomasius' Kenotic Christology

"Kenotic theology can be said to have begun as a serious form of reflection on Christology in the works of Gottfried Thomasius (1802–1875), a German Lutheran theologian."[8] The intellectual milieu in which Thomasius conceived his kenotic Christology was Hegelianism, which affirmed the necessity of the absolute becoming

---

[5] Brito, 2:854.

[6] Brito, 2:854.

[7] Sammie K. Daugherty, *God as Kenosis: Possibilities for Kenotic Theology in the Texts of Robert P. Scharlemann* (Ann Arbor, MI: UMI Dissertations Services, 1998), 9.

[8] Smith, 651.

finite in the historical process of the world so that the absolute could become fully self-actualized. Theologically speaking, for Thomasius, "the primary concern was to find a way of understanding the person of Christ that allowed his *full humanity* to be adequately expressed."[9]

Because of Thomasius' discontent with the traditional language and categories of Chalcedonian Christology, he attempted to do justice to the humanity of Christ by focusing on how God "emptied himself" in the incarnation. Consequently, "some form of kenosis or self-emptying on the part of the Son offered the idea that the Son of God could make himself compatible with finite human existence without giving up the essential ingredients of divinity."[10] This assertion, however, did not place Thomasius outside of the sphere of orthodoxy, for "while Thomasius saw himself as firmly within the ecclesiastical tradition, he [also] recognized that 'the formulations of Chalcedon were apt to suggest two abstract natures and thus fail to achieve a view of an integrated person.'"[11]

Thomasius proceeded to explicate his peculiar version of the *kenosis* by holding three realities in tension: the deity of Christ; the *full* humanity of Christ; and the unity of his person.[12] In fact, "the heart of his system was an attempt to hold all three points together through the notion of self-limitation."[13] With the *kenosis* being the fulcrum of his Christology, Thomasius began by affirming "the reality of the Christian experience of communion with God mediated through Christ,"[14] which entails a soteriology that emphasizes the need for reconciliation between God and humanity as requiring "nothing short of a 'God-man.'"[15]

Thomasius' emphasis on the union of deity and humanity in Jesus stems from his presupposition that "God created man for communion with himself"[16] and for this communion to be restored God needed to take on a full human nature "'in weakness and susceptibility to suffering and trial of its present condition,'

---

[9] Smith, 651. Emphasis mine.
[10] Daugherty, 10.
[11] Daugherty, 11.
[12] Daugherty, 11.
[13] Daugherty, 11–12.
[14] Daugherty, 12.
[15] Daugherty, 12.
[16] Daugherty, 12.

including an openness 'to the influences of wickedness.'"[17] This seemingly scandalous assertion was necessary, according to Thomasius, because

> classical theology had invariably truncated the humanity of Christ in order to protect his divinity. Thomasius believed that if either side was allowed to dominate the other, no true union had occurred. [Therefore], some form of self-limitation on the part of the divine seemed necessary for the union to be genuine.[18]

Thomasius' theory also drew controversy by arguing that, in the *kenosis*, God revealed that he defines himself "in terms of complete self-determination [which] opened up the possibility of attributing a certain type of change to God."[19] The *kenosis*, then, is God's self-determination to be the God he chooses to be regardless of any metaphysical language and/or external forces. Therefore, "when defending the notion of self-limitation, the only justification for God's self-limitation that Thomasius was interested in is the one that protects God's independence."[20] Thus, Thomasius was both a theologian ahead of and immersed in his time because of his recovery of the *kenosis* and adherence to traditional metaphysical presuppositions.

P.T. Forsyth's Kenotic View of Jesus' Pre-Existence and Incarnation

In the wake of the ground-breaking treatment of the *kenosis* by Gottfried Thomasius is the influential thought of Peter Taylor Forsyth, who both succeeded and superseded Thomasius regarding the further development of the *kenosis* in Christology. This was because

> Forsyth's theological background reflected the orthodox Scottish Calvinism of his upbringing. But his studies caused him to challenge much of this, and he came to accept some of what he considered the virtues of liberal theology, particularly biblical criticism.[21]

Because Forsyth drew upon the two streams of orthodox and liberal Protestantism, he could remain within the boundaries of accepted

---

[17] Daugherty, 14.
[18] Daugherty, 14.
[19] Daugherty, 15.
[20] Daugherty, 23.
[21] A.F. Anderson, "Forsyth, Peter Taylor," in *Dictionary of Scottish Church History and Theology*, ed. Nigel Cameron (Downers Grove: InterVarsity Press, 1993), 332.

orthodoxy and yet reformulate, to the extent of revolutionizing, the classical christological confessions, specifically the Formula of Chalcedon. Forsyth, therefore, believed that "the task of Christology is to explicate what must be true about Christ for him to have effected the new relationship between humanity and God. Only an incarnational [and subsequently kenotic] Christology adequately explains that event."[22]

The incarnation of Christ, however, was not the initial "advance in force" for Forsyth, because in order "to explain the finality of Christ, we must believe, as the early church did, in the *pre-existence* of Christ."[23] Unfortunately, the doctrine of the pre-existence of Christ has seemed to be more a matter of rote confessionalism in the life of the church, rather than a dynamic doctrine that would (partially) explain the mystery of the incarnation.

Part of the church's neglect of the pre-existence of Christ was because of the supposed scarcity of *explicit* scriptural passages that testify to its reality, but Forsyth

> claims that the work of Christ cannot be explained without the aid of some theory of His pre-existence. Nothing less takes account of the magnitude of His task, nor does it suffice to explain His divinity. Therefore, although there is little respecting pre-existence in the Scriptures, Forsyth feels compelled to postulate the existence of Christ before the foundation of the world.[24]

The necessity of the doctrine of the pre-existence of Christ is not only to be found in the Scriptures, but is also warranted by its *theological* necessity as part and parcel of a coherent understanding of Christ's person and work. Forsyth points to Paul as one who

> worked back from the faith that all things were made *for* Christ to the conviction that, as the end was in the beginning, all things were made *by* Christ; and by a Christ as personal as the Christ who was their goal. And so, from the exalted glory of Christ, Paul's thought was cast back, by the very working of that Christ in him and in the whole

---

[22] Daugherty, 27.

[23] A.M. Hunter, *P.T. Forsyth* (Philadelphia: Westminster Press, 1974), 76. Author's emphasis.

[24] W.L. Bradley, *P.T. Forsyth: The Man and His Work* (London: Independent Press, 1952), 193.

consciousness of the Church's faith, to the same Christ from all Eternity by the Father's side.[25]

This retrospective theologizing is indicative of the necessity and importance of Christ's pre-existence for Forsyth's kenotic Christology because of his *a priori* commitment "that theology begins from the experience of salvation in Christ. As a consequence, an adequate understanding of Christ requires a right relationship with him."[26]

Furthermore, Forsyth provides two theological rationales for the necessity of the pre-existence of Christ: the eternal relationship between the Father and the Son, and the immutable nature of God. The former is a matter of affirming orthodoxy in which the deity and eternality of the Father and the Son is upheld. "Such a relation as we believe our Saviour now bears to the Father could not have been arisen at a point in time. It could not have been created by this earthly life."[27] The latter is like the former, because God's immutability demands that

> if at one moment in history Christ performed the reconciling work, a change in the nature of God would be necessitated unless there were in that act an eternal aspect thus then becoming actualised. God's nature must be unchangeable, for His holiness guarantees this; nothing which happened within time could be allowed to alter the very character of the Eternal.[28]

Stemming from the argument that the pre-existence of Christ is an absolute necessity in understanding the person and work of Christ, Forsyth proceeds to assert that the *kenosis* began in the pre-existent state of Christ *before* the incarnation. Forsyth believed that "there was an act of renunciation outside the walls of the world and the Son's sacrifice began before he entered it,"[29] and although Christ could not fully complete his substitutionary sacrifice until he assumed human flesh, the *posture* of the pre-existent Son was such

---

[25] P.T. Forsyth, *The Person and Place of Jesus Christ* (London: Independent Press, 1948), 269. Author's emphasis.

[26] Daugherty, 26–27.

[27] Forsyth, *The Person and Place of Jesus Christ*, 269.

[28] Bradley, 194.

[29] Hunter, 76.

that "his sacrifice began before He came into the world, and his cross was that of a lamb slain before the world's foundation."[30]

By positing a view of pre-existence to substantiate that Christ's *kenosis* began before the incarnation, Forsyth could demonstrate that the *kenosis* was not a simple *adjustment* by God in assuming human flesh, but an eternal *act* of self-determination by God to be a God who is essentially *kenotic*:

> The great eternal act of Christ in heaven and Godhead, before and beyond history, was of a like *nature* to the long act of will by which He went down to death in His human history. It was an act of heart and will, of free resolve, of self-limitation, self-contraction as it were, self-divestment, self-humiliation, [and] self-subordination.[31]

The *kenosis*, then, occurred in eternity past in the pre-existence of Christ because of God's self-determination to be a God who chooses to be *for others* and not a God who is self-absorbed and consumed by his own ineffable glory. Therefore,

> Christ's earthly humiliation had to have its foundation laid in Heaven, and to be viewed but as the working out of a renunciation before the world was. The awful volume and power of the will-warfare in which He here redeemed the world, and turned for Eternity the history of the race, was but the exercise in historic conditions of an eternal resolve taken in heavenly places. He could never be king of the eternal future if he was not also king from eternal past.[32]

"It is all but impossible to discuss a question like the Kenosis without entering a region which seems forbidding to the lay mind, and is certainly more or less technical."[33] With this ominous statement, Forsyth begins his treatment on the *kenosis* of Christ as revealed in the incarnation and sets the tone for what has traditionally been a very difficult topic in Christology.

However, for the *kenosis* to be made cognizant in the incarnation of Christ, one must first see the connection between the incarnate and pre-incarnate aspects of the *kenosis*. "Once pre-existence has been accepted as a postulate demanded by religious faith in Christ, it

---

[30] Forsyth, *The Person and Place of Jesus Christ*, 271.

[31] P.T. Forsyth, *The Taste of Death and the Life of Grace* (London: James Clarke & Co., 1901), 111. Author's emphasis.

[32] Forsyth, *The Person and Place of Jesus Christ*, 270.

[33] Forsyth, *The Person and Place of Jesus Christ*, 293.

becomes necessary to deal with the laying aside of the glory of the heavenly Christ and the humiliation of the earthly Christ."[34] This logical connection strengthens Forsyth's argument because "if there was a personal pre-existence in the case of Christ it does not seem possible to adjust it to the historic Jesus without some form of Kenosis."[35]

Forsyth's Moral View of *Kenosis*

Having substantiated the necessity and interdependency of the *kenosis* in Christ's pre-existence and in the incarnation, one must now realize the *moral* nature of the *kenosis*. This "turn to morality" was ingenious because Forsyth saw "his theory [of the *kenosis*] as a biblical alternative to a static, Greek, outmoded formula found in the Chalcedonian Definition."[36] Forsyth believed that this "moralizing of dogma" was necessary in his contemporary context because the traditional "categories and concepts used to explain the incarnation were drawn from abstract and impersonal sources."[37] Moreover, the positive contribution of the "moralizing of dogma" was "the reshaping of our view of God from what [Forsyth] called static categories to dynamic ones reflecting God's saving purposes seen in Christ."[38]

Although Forsyth was in general agreement with the Formula of Chalcedonian, he believed that a new and better explanation of the incarnation would be through *moral*, rather than *metaphysical*, language and categories. Gwilym Griffith aptly states:

> The Chalcedonian formula of the two natures in one Person, designed, as the formula was, for the purpose of dispelling errors rather than for the purpose of adjusting truths, was bound in time to need re-stating. For not only was the formula affected – inevitably – by an early metaphysic and a crude psychology, but also it was framed in a church and in an age in which the moral vitality and urgency of the original Apostolic teaching were lacking, together with that teaching's close relation to personal experience.[39]

---

[34] Robert McAfee Brown, *P.T. Forsyth: Prophet for Today* (Philadelphia: Westminster Press, 1952), 89.

[35] Forsyth, *The Person and Place of Jesus Christ*, 293–294.

[36] Smith, 652.

[37] Daugherty, 27.

[38] Smith, 653.

[39] Gwilym Griffith, *The Theology of P.T. Forsyth* (London: Lutterworth Press, 1948), 38.

Consequently, Forsyth shifted the emphasis from *substance* to *action* by demonstrating that the incarnation, and its subsequent *kenosis*, must not to be understood as "a matter of affirming a logical impossibility, but of affirming a moral choice made by a person to love sacrificially."[40]

Furthermore, in superseding the traditional language and categories of Chalcedonian Christology, Forsyth refuted the traditional view of the *kenosis* as *krypsis*. "The alternative to a Kenosis used to be a Krypsis, or conscious concealment of the active divine glory for practical or strategic purposes. But that is now an impossible idea."[41] The impossibility of holding to the *krypsis* view of the *kenosis* is because, per Forsyth, it "hardly satisfies the exigencies of genuine incarnation. Ultimately, it is docetic. Nor does a veiled divinity do justice to the New Testament witness to the humanity of Christ."[42]

Ultimately, the moral nature of the *kenosis* is the key to understanding both *how* and *why* God became flesh in Jesus of Nazareth, because "any modern Christology, if it is to be religiously true, must concern itself with ethical rather than metaphysical categories and must therefore keep close to the moral and experimental method."[43]

The moral act of the *kenosis* in the incarnation is not an end unto itself, however, but the impetus of the *kenosis* as a *concentration* of the divine attributes in Jesus of Nazareth. The genius of Forsyth's contribution to Christology is seen most clearly in his peculiar approach to delineating the *kenosis* in the incarnation. Simply stated, Forsyth's kenotic Christology posits the notion that "the divine attributes were not parted with but retracted in a different mode of being, becoming *potential* not *actual*."[44]

Because the debate over the nature/extent of the *kenosis* hinges on the role of the divine attributes, it is important to understand that, for Forsyth, "the attributes of God, like omniscience, are not destroyed when they are reduced to a potentiality. They are only

---

[40] Daugherty, 28.

[41] Forsyth, *The Person and Place of Jesus Christ*, 294.

[42] Daugherty, 30–31.

[43] Griffith, 39–40.

[44] Samuel Mikolaski, "P.T. Forsyth," in *Creative Minds in Contemporary Theology*, ed. Philip Edgcumbe Hughes (Grand Rapids: Eerdmans, 1966), 314. Emphasis mine.

concentrated. The self-reduction, or self-retraction, of God might be a better phrase than the self-emptying."[45]

The debate intensifies when the traditional view of God's omniscience in Christ is reformulated by Forsyth's treatment of the *kenosis*. For Forsyth, the omniscience of God "is an intuitive and simultaneous knowledge of all things; but when the Eternal enters time it becomes a discursive and successive knowledge, with the power to know all things only *potential*, and enlarging to become *actual* under the moral conditions that govern human growth and the extension of human knowledge."[46]

For Forsyth, the *kenosis* also entails an ontological necessity in God because "to say that God could not limit himself is itself a limitation on God. The growth and change experienced by Christ in the course of his earthly life, as the natural consequence of his conscious choice to become man, was not a threat to his divinity but an expression of it."[47] Forsyth argues that

> As God, the Son in his freedom would have kenotic power over Himself corresponding to the infinite power of self-determination which belongs to deity. His divine energy and mobility would have a power even to pass into a successive and developing state of being, wherein the consciousness of perfect fulness [*sic*] and changelessness should retire, and become but subliminal or rare... [And] if the Creator could not have become immanent in creation His infinity would have been curtailed by all the powers and dimensions of space. And if immanence could not pass by a new act into incarnation then God would have been lost in his world, and the world lost to God.[48]

The omnipotence of God, then, is revealed most clearly in the *kenosis* of the incarnation meaning that God "is able more than any finite creature to reduce and limit Himself. The possibility of limitation expands the notion of omnipotence, declares Forsyth."[49] What Forsyth intends is to re-think God's *omnipotence* as not sheer, blind power, but as "the power to limit Himself into man [as the] essential part of His infinite power... Limitation or concentration is one of the surest signs of power. Vague power, aimless and wild, is

---

[45] Forsyth, *The Person and Place of Jesus Christ*, 308.
[46] Forsyth, *The Person and Place of Jesus Christ*, 307–308. Emphasis mine.
[47] Daugherty, 32.
[48] Forsyth, *The Person and Place of Jesus Christ*, 310; 314.
[49] Bradley, 201.

not divine."⁵⁰ Therefore, per Forsyth, "a true view of omnipotence would suggest that it does not and cannot do everything a freakish fancy might desire, but only everything that holy love prescribes."⁵¹

Kenosis and the Cross

The final aspect of the *kenosis* in Christ's incarnation is that of the soteriological rationale for the Son "emptying himself." "In Forsyth's view the heart of evangelical faith lies in the message of the cross. Soteriology was even more important for him than Christology, the atonement more crucial than the incarnation."⁵² In fact, as Forsyth states: "It is in redemption that we find the nature of the Incarnation [and *kenosis*],"⁵³ which stems from his presuppositional conviction that "all Christology exists in the interest of the evangelical faith of the layman who has in Jesus Christ the pardon of his sins and everlasting life."⁵⁴

The kenotic Christology of P.T. Forsyth concludes with Christ's *plerosis*, in which he regained his ontological status that he possessed before he chose to "empty himself" before the creation of the world. The *plerosis* is, however, not simply an eternal reward of self-glorification for Christ, but is "the history of his 'moral redintegration,' of his gradual recovery through moral conquest of what he lost in the moral act of becoming human."⁵⁵

The *plerosis* is viewed as a necessary culmination of the entire kenotic movement of God in Christ because "to stop with kenosis is to go but halfway, to be left with the spectacle of a humbled God, but not of a redeeming God."⁵⁶ Forsyth argues that a purely kenotic Jesus could not effect humanity's salvation because for

> redemption we need something more positive. It is a defect in kenotic theories, however sound, that they turn only on one side of the experience of Christ, viz., his descent and humiliation. It is a defect because that renunciatory element is negative after all; and to dwell on it, as modern views of Christ do, is to end in a Christian

---

⁵⁰ Forsyth, *The Taste of Death and the Life of Grace*, 98.

⁵¹ Brown, 91.

⁵² Donald Bloesch, "Forsyth, Peter Taylor," in *Evangelical Dictionary of Theology*, ed. Walter Elwell (Grand Rapids: Baker, 2001), 462.

⁵³ Forsyth, *The Taste of Death and the Life of Grace*, 115.

⁵⁴ Forsyth, *The Person and Place of Jesus Christ*, 9.

⁵⁵ Daugherty, 33–34.

⁵⁶ Brown, 91.

ethic somewhat weak, and tending to ascetic and self-occupied piety... We must keep in view, and keep uppermost, the more positive process, the effective, ascending, and mastering process which went alongside of the renunciation in Christ, nay, was interwoven with it, as its ruling coefficient.[57]

Ultimately, this motif of *redemption* governs Forsyth's doctrine of the *plerosis* because he is concerned to demonstrate the soteriological significance of why God "emptied himself" in Jesus Christ. "Forsyth ever wrote on this theme that he recognized no other guiding principle than Redemption, no other Christocentrism than that which gave central place to Christ as Redeemer."[58] Hence, if one is to possess an adequate view of the person and work of Jesus Christ they must be aware that "the idea of Plerosis helps [them] to understand how Christ was able to fulfill the conditions of human ignorance and temptation, yet transcend them in the final victory of the Cross."[59]

Having established the necessity of holding to a *plerosis* in the entire kenotic movement of God in Christ, one must now realize that Christ "emptied himself" not for himself, but *for humanity*, as evidenced in his moral conquest over sin through his life of overcoming temptation and inevitable death on the cross. "It is Christ's identification with man which is [why] the doctrine of Plerosis [is] so important to Forsyth's study of Christology. The self-fulfillment of Christ becomes our own fulfillment, as we are members of the new Humanity."[60]

Because of Forsyth's disdain for the substance metaphysics of the Chalcedonian Formula, he postulated the idea that Jesus as the *God-man* is best thought of "in terms not of a union of these two natures... but of a union of these two personal *movements*. In the historic life of Christ the two *movements* – perfect revelation and perfect religion – were united, involuted."[61] Therefore, when applied to the *kenosis-plerosis* paradigm, one sees that "the Kenosis

---

[57] Forsyth, *The Person and Place of Jesus Christ*, 329.

[58] Griffith, 43.

[59] Bradley, 205.

[60] Bradley, 204.

[61] Hunter, 78. Emphasis mine.

represents God's movement towards man, while Plerosis manifests man's movement towards God."[62]

Having already established the *kenosis* as God's movement towards humanity in Christ as revealed in the incarnation, the *plerosis* began to actualize in the cruciform life of Christ. Forsyth argues that Jesus' "growth in grace was the history of the world's moral crisis, [and] it was, in the same act, the growth of our salvation; for the atoning cross was the principle and the achievement of his whole moral life."[63] Therefore, as an involution of the divine and human "movements," Jesus' *plerosis* was contingent upon the positive development of his morality, for "the more he laid down his personal life the more he gained his divine soul. The more his divine soul renounced his immunities [from temptation] the more he acquired of glory."[64]

Christ's *plerosis*, then, was a moral conquest for the forgiveness of sins because "redemption was a *spiritual* conflict and victory in a great *moral* war."[65] Because God always acts morally, his salvation is moral in nature, which means that "the story of Christ's incarnate life of growth becomes the story of his recovery, by moral conquest, of that mode of being from which, by a tremendous moral act, he came. This is *plerosis*."[66]

According to Forsyth, the superlative and final act by which the *plerosis* was completed was in the crucifixion, and although Jesus overcame the temptation to sin during his earthly life and ministry, this strenuous emphasis on the cross "buttresses Forsyth's opinion that the person of Christ is to be interpreted by His work, since it is at the Cross that Jesus finally achieves the highest development of His life."[67] Furthermore, in emphasizing the cross as the pinnacle of Christ's self-realization of his identity and mission, Forsyth declares that "it was not till he died that he possessed his whole soul, came to his own, entered on all he really was… and could teach about himself things impossible before."[68]

---

[62] Bradley, 207.

[63] Forsyth, *The Person and Place of Jesus Christ*, 348.

[64] Forsyth, *The Person and Place of Jesus Christ*, 349.

[65] Forsyth, *The Taste of Death and the Life of Grace*, 114–115. Author's emphasis.

[66] Hunter, 78.

[67] Bradley, 205.

[68] Forsyth, *The Person and Place of Jesus Christ*, 121–122.

The *kenosis* of Christ, which of ontological necessity began in his pre-existence, continued into his incarnation as a concentration of his divine attributes, and provided the necessary conditions for his *plerosis* through cruciform moral conquest, "is a doctrine which does full justice to the moral miracle of the God-man. [For] in Christ we are bidden to see One who, for love of sinful man, renounced the high glories of heaven to become man, taking a servant's form, and who by his life of perfect obedience to his heavenly Father, even unto death on the cross, gained for himself the highest place that heaven affords."[69]

---

[69] Hunter, 80.

'Zeig uns durch deine Passion':
The Christology of Bach's St John Passion

Andreas Loewe

St Paul's Cathedral Melbourne
Melbourne Conservatorium of Music

Introduction

On a wet, early spring afternoon, on Good Friday 1724, the congregants of Leipzig's Nikolaikirche witnessed the first performance of Bach's *St John Passion*.[1] For at least a generation, Good Friday in Leipzig's principal Lutheran churches—St Thomas', St Nikolai and the 'New' Church—had concluded with the singing of Johann Walter's chanted Passion.[2] As part of the final liturgical observance of the day, the story of the death of Jesus would be sung, combining words and music in order to reflect on the significance of that day.

Bach took the proclamation of the cross to a new level – theologically and musically. Rather than use a poetic retelling of the Passion story as his textual basis, Bach made use of a single gospel account, matched with contemporary poems and traditional chorales to retell the trial and death of Jesus. By providing regular opportunities for theological reflection, he purposefully created a "sermon in sound" and so, in his music making, he closely mirrors Lutheran Baroque homiletic principles.

An orthodox Lutheran believer throughout his life, Bach's Passion serves as a vehicle to invite his listeners to make their own his belief that it was "through Christ's agony and death" that "all the world's

---

[1] Andreas Elias Büchner, Johann Kanold, *Vollständiges und accurates Universal-Register, Aller wichtigen und merckwürdigen Materien* (Erfurt: Jungnicol, 1736), 680.

[2] As popularised in Gottfried Vopelius, ed., *Neu Leipziger Gesangbuch/ Von den schönsten und besten Liedern verfasset/ In welchem Nicht allein des sel. Herrn D. Lutheri und andere mit Gottes Wort/ und unveränderter Augsburgischer Confession überein stimmende... und gebräuchliche Gesänge/ Lateinische Hymni und Psalmen/ Mit 4. 5. bis 6. Stimmen/ deren Melodeyen Theils aus Johann Herman Scheins Cantional, und andern guten Autoribus zusammen getagen/ theils aber selbsten componiret... / Mit Fleiß verfertiget und herausgegeben von Gottfried Vopelio* (Leipzig: Christoph Klinger, 1682).

redemption" had come.³ Bach's intent is to take his listeners on a musical journey to the cross and beyond. As they journey, he provides regular pointers to enable the hearers to see beyond the Man of Sorrows and recognise in the broken, human Jesus, the self-emptying, saving Christ. The principal aim, then, of Bach's musical sermon was to instil in his listeners a sense of gratitude for the saving death of Christ, and to kindle in their hearts a response of loving affection.

Using the theological writings of the German reformer Martin Luther as a theological foundation, Bach encourages his listeners to make their own the response to Christ's death Luther himself had set out in 1522: "When I recognise the death of Christ for me I must love him in return, for one must respond in love to such a man".⁴ At the end of his Passion, Bach's listeners are left not with a sense of loss and grief but with a sense of acceptance and fulfilment: the empty cross is a sign of salvation, the tomb is the temporary resting place of the Son of God. In the same way, those who followed Christ in discipleship would rest until they, too, shared his resurrection.⁵

At the heart of the Passion story stands the insight that a gracious God showed his mercy by "emptying himself, taking on the form of a servant, being born in human likeness", and as true human and true God to humble himself further "by becoming obedient to the point of death, even death on a cross" (Phil 2:6–8). For the reformer Martin Luther, the appropriate response to the kenotic event of the cross was the believers' confession of, and love for, Christ. It is in their loving confession that they partake of *theopoieosis*: "Ascend beyond the Son to the Father and I see that Christ is God and that he has plunged himself into my death, my sin, my misery and in

---

[3] Johann Sebastian Bach, *Johannespassion BWV 245*, no. 32: "Mein teurer Heiland, lass dich fragen", cited in Andreas Loewe, *Johann Sebastian Bach's St John Passion (BWV 245): A Theological Commentary* (Leiden: Brill, 2014), 129: "Kann ich durch deine Pein und Sterben/ das Himmelreich ererben?/ Ist aller Welt Erlösung da?" (Can I through your agony and death/ The kingdom of heaven inherit?/ Is all the world's redemption there?).

[4] Martin Luther, *D. Martin Luthers Werke: Kritische Gesamtausgabe* [hereafter WA], ed. Joachim Karl Friedrich Knaake et al. (Weimar, 1883–1985), *Sermon von der Tröstung des heiligen Geistes in der Verfolgung 1522*, 10 III: 154, 18–19: "So ich das erkenne, so müß ich in widerumb liebhaben, Dann ainem solchen man müß ich hold sein".

[5] Loewe, *St John Passion*, 96.

this way gives me his grace".[6] The libretto Bach sets to music is a deliberate reflection on this kenotic arc: at the very beginning of the Passion stands the conviction that this work will demonstrate, *zeig uns*, that God in Christ was glorified in deepest lowliness, *in der größten Niedrigkeit*.[7]

Luther's Theology: Expressing the Reformation Message through Music

Both the form and the theological basis for Bach's musical Passion sermon are founded on the theology of Martin Luther. The German reformer held that music was "next to theology".[8] While he was by no means the first to discover the power of music to stimulate the imagination, he certainly was one of the first church leaders to harness music as a means to tell the Gospel story (and, as his movement gained momentum across Germany, the story of the reformation) through songs, hymns, and devotional plays.[9] A musician himself, Luther understood the power of the sung word: it was a means "to speak and preach of the promise and grace of God so that others might come to hear of it and partake of it... and to incite people to do good, and teach them".[10]

The first century of Luther's reformation led to a multi-genre artistic explosion that principally centred on Luther's great theological breakthroughs: his insight that justification was by grace alone, and his theology of the cross which flowed from it. Luther had first postulated his theology of salvation in his 1517 *Ninety-Five Theses against Indulgences*.[11] By 1519 Luther resoundingly affirmed that:

---

[6] Luther, *Sermon von der Tröstung des heiligen Geistes in der Verfolgung 1522*, WA 10 III: 154, 19–155, 1: "Steyge ich weyter am sun auffyhn zum vater und sehe das Christus got sey und hab sich in meinen todt, in mein sünde, in mein ellende gesteckt, und gibt mir auch sein hulde".

[7] Bach, *BWV 245*, no. 1: "Herr, unser Herrscher", cited in Loewe, *St John Passion*, 141.

[8] Luther, *Tischreden* [hereafter WA Tr] 6: 348, 22–4, no. 7034: "Ich gebe nach der Theologie der Musica den nähesten Locum und höchste Ehre".

[9] For Lutheran popular drama and educational plays, see: Andreas Loewe, "Proclaiming the Passion: Popular Drama and the Passion Tradition in Luther's Germany", *Reformation and Renaissance Review* 12.2/3 (2010), 235–82.

[10] Luther, *Von den letzten Worten Davids 1543*, WA 54: 33, 18–22: "Redet und prediget von solcher verheissung und gnade Gottes, das ander Leute auch dazu komen, und der teilhaftig werden... auch die menschen nützlich zu reitzen und zu leren".

[11] Luther, *Disputatio pro declaration virtutis indulgentiarum 1517*, WA 1: 238, 18.

"CRUX sola est nostra Theologia".[12] From then on, his understanding of the centrality of the cross for justification would pervade his entire theology, in particular his Christology. For Luther, "God can be found in no other way than the Passion and the cross".[13]

It is through Christ's death and resurrection that both the hypostatic union and the distinction of Christ's two natures are best shown forth: Christ's divine nature is hidden in the human; the cross hides the resurrection; weakness hides the power of God. While these hidden realities will not be completely revealed until the Second Coming, their effects are already being made present. Calvary was the final expression of the kenotic journey of the eternal God to take away human sin: in Jesus' human powerlessness, God's true power is shown forth; overcoming the world and the power of evil. As Luther explained: "On the cross Christ was powerless, yet there he performed his mightiest work: conquering sin, death, world, hell, devil and all evil".[14]

In 1522 Luther reflected on this cosmic redemptive work in terms of the *communicatio idiomatum*: "what Christ accomplishes or suffers, God surely has accomplished and suffered, even though the same only was experienced by one nature".[15] Not only is God manifested in the midst of our human lives through the cross; his self-offering, sacrifice and exaltation, his plunging the depth of our existence and sharing our death saves humankind and exalts human nature into God's presence: "For ultimately, all that is said about Christ's humiliation and exaltation shall be accorded to humanity", Luther affirms.[16]

For the reformer, the suffering and death on the cross of the Man of Sorrows fully reveals the glory of the hidden God. Luther

---

[12] Luther, *Operationes in Psalmos 1519–21*, WA 5: 176, 32–3: "The cross alone is our theology".

[13] Luther, *Disputatio Heidelbergae habita 1518*, WA 1: 362, 28–29: "At Deum non inveniri nisi in passionibus et cruce".

[14] Luther, *Das Magnificat verdeutschet und ausgelegt 1521*, WA 7: 586, 15–17: "Sihe, alzo wart Christus krafftlos am Creutz, und eben da selb thet er die groste macht, ubirwand die sund, tod, welt, helle, teuffel und allis ubel".

[15] Luther, *Kirchenpostille 1522*, WA 10 I/1: 150, 22–23: "Was Christus thut odder leydet, hatt gewißlich gott than unnd gelieden, wiewol doch nur eyner natur dasselb begegnett ist".

[16] Luther, *Kirchenpostille 1522*, WA 10 I/1: 150, 8–10: "Und endlich alles, was von Christus nydrung unnd erhohung ist gesagt, soll dem menschen tzugelegt werden".

summarised this paradox as follows: "A human hides his own things in order to conceal them, God hides his own things in order to reveal them".[17] In this way, God demonstrates his true glory in the abject humiliation of the cross, and there is proclaimed for all time as Lord of all.

Lutheran Christology in Bach's St John Passion

Luther's christological insights provide the theological framework for Bach's Passion. He opens his work with an imposing chorale proclaiming Christ's self-emptying. Bach's singers call on the God made man: "Show us through your Passion/ that you, the true Son of God,/ for all time,/ even in the deepest lowliness,/ have been made noble".[18] The very opening words of the Passion, then, act as a theological guide for his listeners as they journey to the cross. They encourage listeners to look beyond the man "who was for us, at night,/ trapped as a thief,/ led before godless people,/ and falsely accused,/ laughed at, ridiculed, spat at", and instead to behold in this image of broken humanity in a broken world the "heavenly image" of the true Son of God who has conquered this world.[19]

From the outset of the Passion listeners are invited to react to the events that follow by a personal response of faith and love, knowing that by their faithful, devotional participation in the Passion, they may come to perceive what the "theologians of glory" will never comprehend:[20] that divine power is displayed in weakness, and that "God deliberately chooses to be made known in the Passion and cross".[21] Having taken his listener beyond the cross of Christ to his

---

[17] Luther, *Sermo Die Sancti Matthiae Anno 1517*, WA 1: 138, 13–15: "Homo abscondit sua ut neget: Deus abscondit sua ut revelet".

[18] Bach, *BWV 245*, no. 1: "Herr, unser Herrscher", cited in Loewe, *St John Passion*, 141: "Zeig uns durch deine Passion,/ dass du, der wahre Gottessohn,/ zu aller Zeit,/ auch in der größten Niedrigkeit,/ verherrlicht worden bist".

[19] Bach, *BWV 245*, no. 15: "Christus, der uns selig macht", cited in Loewe, *St John Passion*, 184: "der ward für uns in der Nacht, als ein Dieb gefangen,/ geführt für gottlose Leut,/ und fälschlich verklaget,/ verlacht, verhöhnt und verspeit". Luther, *Ein Sermon von der Bereitung zum Sterben 1519*, WA 2: 691, 19; "Das hymelisch bild".

[20] Luther, *Disputatio Heidelbergae habita 1518*, WA 1: 362, 11–14: "Thus it is never enough nor does it profit anyone who regards God in glory and majesty and does not recognise him in the humility and ignominy of the cross. In this way 'I will destroy the wisdom of the wise etc.' [1 Cor 1:19]. As Isaiah says: 'Truly you are a hidden God' [Isa 45:15]." (Ita ut nulli iam satis sit ac prosit, qui cognoscit Deum in gloria et maiestate, nisi cognoscat eundem in humilitate et ignominia crucis. Sic perdit sapientiam sapientum &c sicut Isaias dicit: Vere absconditus tu es Deus).

[21] Loewe, *St John Passion*, 95.

three-day sepulchre, Bach invites his hearers to "believe that Jesus is the Messiah, the Son of God, and that through believing you may have life in his name" (Jn 20:31), following the express intent of the Fourth Evangelist.

Bach's Passion concludes with a resounding affirmation of the Lordship of Christ, who saves from death and so has brought humanity into the Godhead. In the final bars of the Passion, the crucified, entombed Jesus is revealed to be the conqueror of death and harrower of hell. As the listeners hear the choir sing their confession of the giver of new life, they are encouraged to make their prayer their own and recognise Christ to be both Saviour of the world, and Saviour of their own lives: "Thereupon from death awake me,/ that my eyes may see you in all joy,/ O Son of God,/ my Saviour and my throne of grace,/ Lord Jesus Christ".[22]

Within this frame of opening chorus and closing chorale, Bach retells the story of the cross to enable the listener to arrive at the same faith-filled response that he places on the lips of his singers: that the hidden God is fully revealed in his saving work on the cross, and his glory is shown forth by the death of his only-begotten incarnate Son. Three musical examples, one chorus and two chorales, seek to illustrate how Bach set this theological framework to music. We have previously referred to two of them: the magisterial opening chorus, *Herr, unser Herrscher* (Lord, our Lord) and the concluding chorale, *Ach Herr, lass dein lieb Engelein* (O Lord, let your lovely little angels).

The third example, found about two-thirds through the work, is the chorale *In meines Herzens Grunde* (In the depths of my heart).[23] It concludes Bach's re-telling of Jesus' trial before Pilate, and leads into his retelling of the crucifixion. Each provide a musical reflection on the significance of Christ's sacrificial act on the cross: the opening chorale considers the kenotic exchange of God's divine glory for abject human humiliation, the concluding chorale affirms the certainty of life restored through Christ's death on the cross, while the middle chorale centres on the emotional impact of the Passion on each listener. We will consider these in chronological

---

[22] Bach, *BWV 245*, no. 40: "Ach Herr, lass dein lieb Engelein", cited in Loewe, *St John Passion*, 295: "Alsdenn vom Tod erwecke mich,/ Daß meine Augen sehen dich/ In aller Freud, o Gottes Sohn,/ Mein Heiland und Genadenthron!/ Herr Jesu Christ".

[23] Bach, *BWV 245*, no. 26: "In meines Herzens Grunde", cited in Loewe, *St John Passion*, 256.

order, in the same way in which they are experienced in a performance of the work.

1. Herr, unser Herrscher (Lord, our Lord):

Bach opens his work with a powerful reflection on the glory of the triune God. Following a portentous instrumental introduction by woodwind and flutes, the choir sings the praises of God, echoing words from Psalm 8: "Lord, our God, how glorious is your name in all the world" (Psa 8:1). *Herr, unser Herrscher, dessen Ruhm in allen Landen herrlich ist* (Lord, our Lord, whose fame in all lands is noble). Three times the choir calls out to God as "Lord", each call is interspersed by a crotchet's rest (a rest of a single note), reinforcing the theological understanding of the triune God as three persons, and therefore the Passion as an act of salvation wrought by the Trinity.

God is glorified through all the earth. He is *herrlich*, "noble", as well as Herr, "Lord". For Bach, God's nobility and Lordship is most closely shown forth in the incarnation of Christ, and his kenosis by becoming human and suffering a human death. A number of commentators on Bach's instrumentation suggest that the restless sequence of cadences in the strings is a reflection in music on the restlessness of the human condition, perhaps echoing the thought of St Augustine that "our hearts are restless, until they find their rest in you".[24] Romantic readers of the work, including Bach's first serious biographer Philipp Spitta, heard giant waves in the opening bars that tossed human souls about in a restless ocean of life – reflecting on the *Anfechtungen* of life.[25] Whatever the precise musical intent – whether restlessness or *Anfechtungen* – God enters into the human condition: he is only truly our *Herrscher*, is genuinely made *herrlich* only at the point at which he is made human. As the choir echoes the restless pattern of the strings, it proclaims that God is the triune Lord made noble in humanity. God's Word becomes flesh, tabernacles among us, and will reveal his glory on the cross, Bach amplifies in music the central themes of the Fourth Gospel.

The opening woodwind lines introduce a recurrent musical device that is central to the music of the Passion. Bach not only writes

---

[24] Augustine, *Confessionum, libri tredecim*, ed. P. Knöll (Leipzig: Teubner, 1898) [CSEL 33] 1.1: "inquietum est cor nostrum, donec requiescat in te".

[25] Philipp Spitta, *Johann Sebastian Bach*, 2 vols (Leipzig: Breitkopf und Härtel, 1873–1880), 2: 365.

music to hear, but "music for the eyes", *Augenmusik*. Baroque music, like other Baroque art, thrived on such embedded messages. Bach here introduces the "cross motif", a symbol of the cross, to embed a perpetual focus of the journey of faith into his score.[26] The cross extends across both woodwind lines, is clearly visible in the score and, some commentators suggest, can even be heard because of its jarring dissonance. From the first two bars of the work, therefore, the destination of the musical journey is evident: the climax and turning point of this musical drama is the crucifixion of the Son of God. While the chorus still sings of the glory of God shown forth in the incarnation, the oboes and flutes already give voice to the suffering and sacrifice of God on the cross.

This first movement of the Passion, then, is rich in musical imagery: Bach's threefold exclamatory proclamation of God as the triune Lord is echoed by four choral fugal entries on *Zeig uns durch deine Passion* (Show us through your Passion), entreating the hidden God to reveal himself to the faithful in his work of salvation. Four matching entries set to music the words, *dass du, der wahre Gottessohn* (that you, the true Son of God). The opening proclamation and fugue highlight the insight that Christ was first glorified in his incarnation, and revealed as the God of glory in his debasement on the cross. The way in which "the true Son of God" has been made noble for all time was "in the deepest lowliness". The nobility or glory that Christ gains is by taking on him human form and human suffering and so, when the choir sings of the way in which Christ is *verherrlicht* in the Passion, Bach again makes use of the restless semiquaver lines of the strings, in order to emphasise Christ's complete acceptance of the human condition.

Bach's opening movement affirms how God's act of salvation is indeed one of self-revelation. Just as the death of Christ reveals three persons of the Trinity acting in harmony to effect the redemption of humankind – the death of the incarnate Son subsuming all human sin, making satisfaction to the Father, and effecting, at the giving up his own breath, the sending out of the Holy Spirit – so here Bach invokes the three persons of the Trinity to be present in this act of devotion, and so to be made present in the lives of the worshippers.

---

[26] For earlier uses of such a motif, in particular in Heinrich Schütz's *St John Passion*, see Tamsin D. Jones, *Passions in Perspective: An Analytical Discussion of the three Passion Settings of Heinrich Schütz (1585–1672) against their Historical and Stylistic Backgrounds* (Unpublished Doctoral Dissertation: Birmingham University, 2000), 212, 234.

2. In meines Herzens Grunde:

The use of a well-known funeral chorale, *In meines Herzens Grunde* (In the depth of my heart), aims to anchor the events of Calvary in the lives of the worshipping community. Christ's holy name and his cross are set up as ensigns in the heart of each believer, the chorale proclaims. There they glow as lights of hope in the darkness of human adversity: they literally *funkeln* (sparkle) as bright as rock crystals or diamonds under a bright sun. The invocation of Christ's name and the remembrance of his cross are both a defence against evil, and consolation in *Anfechtung*. Because of their inherent salvific power, *drauf' kann ich fröhlich sein* (I can be cheerful).[27]

Luther had reflected on this "image of grace" or *Gnadenbild* in 1519 in much the same way:

> This is grace and mercy: that on the cross Christ has taken away your sin; that he carries your sin for you and crushes it for you. And that those who firmly believe this, and have this image before their inner eyes, do not doubt this. That is what it means to gaze on the image of grace and to set it up within oneself.[28]

Following Luther, for Bach the proper way to respond to the crucifixion is by internalising the events of Calvary, by enshrining the cross as a means of personal salvation. Those who take the events of the cross into their own hearts, Bach expresses in music, will "for all time and at all hours" have confidence and consolation in their own undoubted adversity, because they will know that it was for them that Christ, their Lord, "so charitable... [has] bled to death".[29]

This is the ground of their believing: Bach's play of words on *Grund* in the German libretto enables a reflection on all of the word's literal senses. *Grund* here means both "reason" and "depth" as well as "field". The image of the cross is the ground of all faith and, when set up in the depth of human hearts, functions very much like a standard or ensign set up on a battlefield. The image of the cross

---

[27] Bach, *BWV 245*, no. 26: "In meines Herzens Grunde", cited in Loewe, *St John Passion*, 256.

[28] Luther, *Ein Sermon von der Bereitung zum Sterben 1519*, WA 2: 686, 33–35: "Das ist gnade und barmhertzickeit, das Christus am Creutz deyne sund von dir nymmet, tregt sie fur dich und erwurget sie, und dasselb festiglich glauben und vor augen haben, nit drann zweyfellnn, das heyst das gnaden bild ansehen und ynn sich bilden".

[29] Bach, *BWV 245*, no. 26: "In meines Herzens Grunde", cited in Loewe, *St John Passion*, 256: "Du, Herr Christ, so milde/ Dich hast geblut' zu Tod!"

enshrined in the human heart is at once a symbol of public allegiance to Christ and a sign of the cosmic effects of the cross, as it is an intimate, personal image of profoundly cherished reassurance.

Believers may claim the redemptive work of Christ, his power of goodness, when faced with any evil, by taking on them *dein Nam* and so are known as Christ's own forever. They may make present Christ's power over death at the hour of their own deaths by enshrining the image of the cross in their hearts. In this way the instrument of death becomes a symbol of life, as the German theologian Johannes Olearius expressed in his *Biblische Erklärung* (a copy of which Bach owned and bequeathed to his son Friedemann):[30]

> This shows/ that the death of our Saviour is the end of all suffering/ the principal purpose of which is our consolation/ that Christ's death may be for us our life/ and that the death that he suffered on our behalf/ has in this way become for us merely a slumber.[31]

3. Ach Herr, lass dein lieb Engelein:

Bach's Passion concludes with an intimate confession of commitment to Christ. In the final chorale of the Passion, the believer is no longer placed on a battlefield between good and evil, death and life, as in the previous example. In his final chorale Bach confidently affirms the belief, expressed in the opening chorale, that the triune God has fully made himself known by letting the incarnate Son be killed on a cross so that his glory may be established for all times.

All is now completed: Christ has died and has conquered death. In giving up his spirit on the cross, he sent out the Spirit that will renew the world. Even the grave is now hallowed. The three-day sepulchre "makes Heaven open/ and Hell shut to me".[32] For those

---

[30] See *Specificatio der Verlassenschaft des am 28. July 1750 verstorbenen Herrn Johann Sebastian Bachs*, in Werner Neumann and Hans Joachim Schulze, eds., *Bach-Dokumente*, 3 vols (Kassel: Bärenreiter, 1963–1972), 2, no. 627. For the Lutheran theological works owned by Bach, see Robin A. Leaver, "Bach und die Lutherschriften seiner Bibliothek", in *Bach-Jahrbuch* 61 (1975), 124–132.

[31] Johannes Olearius, *Haupt Schlüßel der Gantzen Heiligen Schrift... Fünfter und letzter Teil/ Darinnen das gantze/ Neue/ Testament* (Leipzig: Chr. Tarnoven, 1681), 783: "Weiset/ daß der Todt unsers Heylandes sey das Ende alles Leidens/ dess Haupt-Zweck ist unser Trost/ daß der Todt Christi sey unser Leben/ und was Er als einen Todt für uns erduldet hat/ dasselbe ist uns nunmehr ein Schlaff worden".

[32] Bach, *BWV 245*, no. 39: "Ruht wohl", cited in Loewe, *St John Passion*, 292: "Macht mir den Himmel auf/ und schließt die Hölle zu".

who are willing to make Bach's beliefs their own, there is no more fear of death, for Christ sanctifies our own deaths. As Luther had expressed:

> Christ's sepulchre is… our treasure, by which we are sanctified through and through from our sins. It is the treasure by which we have received everything: forgiveness of sins, death and all misfortune.[33]

At the end of the Passion, as at its beginning, stands a prayer. Where the first movement of the Passion entreated the blessed Trinity to reveal itself as the God who is glorified through *kenosis*, this prayer addresses the conqueror of the grave. Echoing the parable of the rich man and Lazarus in Luke's Gospel (Lk 16:19-31), the chorale asks that at the end of the singer's life, Christ would send his holy angels to carry the departed soul into Abraham's bosom. Comforted by the certainty that through "his death and grave [Christ] has killed and buried my sin, and that of all who believe in him", death and judgement have lost its thrall.[34]

So diminished are the powers of death and evil that life's end is gentle falling asleep as in one's own bedchamber, while Christ's judgement is filled with grace, *gar sanft ohn alle Qual und Pein* (gently, without any torment or agony at all), for those who believe this good news.[35] At the end stands not perpetual death but a glorious resurrection for all who call on Christ as their Saviour: *mein Heiland und Genadenthron* (my Saviour and throne of mercy). Those who call on Christ regard him not as the Man of Sorrows, but behold him as the Son of God, who has come to bring joy and delight, and who delights in receiving the praises of his people, which is why Bach's prayer and his Passion appropriately conclude with words of praise: *Ich will dich preisen ewiglich* (I want to praise you forever).[36]

---

[33] Luther, *Wochenpredigten über Johannes 1528–29*, WA 28: 420, 23–27: "Christus Grab ist… unser Schatz… dadurch wir durch and durch geheiliget sein von unsern Sünden, und in welchem Schatz wir alles haben. Nemlich Erlösung von Sünd, Tod und allem Unglück".

[34] Idem, WA 28: 420, 28–29: "Das durch sein Tod und Grab meine und aller die an In gleuben, Sünde getödtet und begraben würden".

[35] Loewe, *St John Passion*, 298.

[36] Loewe, *St John Passion*, 134.

Conclusion

Bach's St John Passion is so effective as a work of Christian devotion, because it elicits a response to the message of the cross. We have seen that Bach is an expert translator of Luther's doctrine into music: his work skilfully augments the Johannine Passion narrative, and the wider incarnational concerns of the Fourth Evangelist by weaving into his musical construct echoes of Luther's own thought: through Scripture and poetry as in our first musical example and, as in the second and third, through the living tradition of Lutheran worship.

The Christology of Bach's *St John Passion* is therefore Luther's Christology, retold through Scripture, devotional poetry and the purpose-written hymns and anthems that reflect on the theology of Luther's reformation; a combination that surely would have delighted the reformer, had he been able to witness it. Bach sets to music the conviction that a distant, hidden God may be revealed to the believer to be a gracious, personal Saviour. That those who accept this message will find consolation, hope and confidence for their own lives through the cross. As in a Lutheran sermon, Bach invites his listeners to put their trust in this triune God. They are invited to recognise the glory that flows from the cross, the joy that can be found in the conquered grave, and the life that can be enjoyed in discipleship of this Saviour both here and hereafter.

As the Passion concluded, the congregants of St Nikolai went on their way home into the dusk of a wet spring evening. Signs of new life abounded around them. Bach left them with the invitation to come and share his belief that the cross was a new beginning, not the end. For the composer his passion to communicate in music the good news of the cross would lead him to write at least one, if not two, further Passions; the great Passion, performed the following year, giving voice to the story of the self-emptying Son of God through St Matthew's eyes.

Welcoming Strangers in the Name of Christ: Abraham Kuyper and the Ethics of Political Discipleship

Michael Bräutigam

Melbourne School of Theology

> When the Son of Man comes in his glory, and all the angels with him, then he will sit on his glorious throne. Before him will be gathered all the nations, and he will separate people one from another as a shepherd separates the sheep from the goats. And he will place the sheep on his right, but the goats on the left. Then the King will say to those on his right, 'Come, you who are blessed by my Father, inherit the kingdom prepared for you from the foundation of the world. For I was hungry and you gave me food, I was thirsty and you gave me drink, I was a stranger and you welcomed me, I was naked and you clothed me, I was sick and you visited me, I was in prison and you came to me.' Then the righteous will answer him, saying, 'Lord, when did we see you hungry and feed you, or thirsty and give you drink? And when did we see you a stranger and welcome you, or naked and clothe you? And when did we see you sick or in prison and visit you?' And the King will answer them, 'Truly, I say to you, as you did it to one of the least of these my brothers, you did it to me.' (Matt 25:31–40)[1]

Europe is faced with the most severe crisis after the Second World War. Over a million refugees arrived last year in Germany alone.[2] Official figures vary as no one really knows the correct number of migrants who crossed the borders overland in Southeast Europe or across the Mediterranean Sea. And we, observing the events from afar, are shocked when we read the stories of those who did not make it over the border alive. Who could ever forget the picture of the drowned Syrian boy who was washed up on the Turkish beach last year.[3] It was shortly after this incident that German chancellor

---

[1] All Scripture quotations, unless otherwise indicated, are taken from *The Holy Bible, English Standard Version®* (ESV®), Copyright © 2001 by Crossway, a publishing ministry of Good News Publishers. All rights reserved.

[2] Cf. http://www.bbc.com/news/world-europe-34131911, accessed 30 January 2016; http://www.welt.de/politik/deutschland/article150678614/1-1-Millionen-Fluechtlinge-kamen-2015-nach-Deutschland.html, accessed 2 February 2016.

[3] See, for example, http://www.theguardian.com/world/2015/sep/02/shocking-image-of-drowned-syrian-boy-shows-tragic-plight-of-refugees, accessed 29 March 2016.

Angela Merkel had one of her rare emotional outbursts: "If we are now supposed to apologize for the fact that we are showing a friendly face in this emergency situation," Merkel said, "then this isn't my country anymore."[4] The Protestant minister's daughter here responded to critics in her own party who tried to force her to either close the borders or at least introduce an upper limit for refugee numbers that would be acceptable to Germany. What we are currently witnessing in Europe is a crisis on multiple levels.

There is, *first*, of course the plight of the refugees, many of them Christians, who try to escape Bashar al-Assad's regime or ISIS' terror, and who risk their lives as they flee to the European continent. *Secondly*, this crisis has plunged the European Union into unprecedented chaos; its member countries disagree on a quota system which could regulate a fair distribution of refugees: member states in the east (e.g. Poland, Czech Republic, Slovakia) are less willing to welcome refugees than those in the north or south (Germany, France, Spain, Italy).[5] *Thirdly*, this crisis challenges societal cohesion in Europe. The more migrants arrive, the greater the need for integration. While the volunteers in refugee centers in major European cities still outnumber those who try to burn them down, pressure is mounting and right-wing parties are gaining considerable support. How are Christians to react in light of this multiple crisis? After all, are we—as members of the body of Christ—not called "salt of the earth" and the "light of the world" (Matt 5:13–14)? Yet are we, really?

My aim in this essay is *not* to discuss the macro level of world politics but to zoom in on the mission of the Christian Church and its individual members. I am convinced that the Christian Church is a central part of the solution to the refugee crisis. This crisis calls for a new generation of Christian disciples who are active members of society, who love neighbor and enemy, and contribute to the flourishing of human communities. In short, we need radical followers of Christ who are willing to adopt what Graham Ward has termed the "politics of discipleship."[6] In what follows, we are

---

[4] Cf. http://www.spiegel.de/international/germany/refugee-policy-of-chancellor-merkel-divides-europe-a-1053603.html, accessed 10 February 2016.

[5] Cf. http://www.welt.de/politik/ausland/article151706915/Diese-Laender-haben-bisher-keinen-Fluechtling-aufgenommen.html, accessed 29 March 2016.

[6] Graham Ward strongly emphasized the "call to political discipleship for Christians." Ward, *The Politics of Discipleship: Becoming Postmaterial Citizens* (London: SCM Press, 2009), 39.

going to explore the key characteristics of twenty-first century political disciples and the way they respond to the present refugee crisis. I intend to proceed as follows: As a first step, we will examine the radical nature of the call into discipleship and the political nature of the disciples. In a second step, we will focus on Abraham Kuyper's contribution, which in my view offers concrete suggestions as to how political discipleship could be effectively implemented today.

Loving God and Neighbor

A professor of theology once asked Jesus, "Of all the commandments, which is the most important?" (Mk 12:28). Evidently, in the jungle of Jewish laws even an expert could sometimes lose track of what was really significant and what was not. Jesus' answer was clear and crisp: "'Love the Lord your God with all your heart and with all your soul and with all your mind and with all your strength.' The second is this: 'Love your neighbor as yourself.' There is no commandment greater than these." (Mk 12:30–31). To love God and to love neighbor is what Jesus demands from his disciples. This second commandment seems particularly challenging to members of the human race. "But who is my neighbor?" another theology expert wants to know (Lk 10:29). And Jesus does what he often does when he is asked a question: he tells a story.

This is the story where someone travels from Jerusalem to Jericho and is robbed, severely beaten, and left behind in a serious condition. A priest comes by, sees the injured man, but he passes on the other side of the road. Next, another Jewish religious leader, a Levite, comes down the road. Although he takes a closer look, he too passes on the other side of the road and fails to offer help. Then, a Samaritan comes by, and Jesus' Jewish audience would have expected the Samaritan to be the least likely one to get involved (the Jews did not think much of the Samaritans). However, the climax of Jesus' story is that this Samaritan is a *good* Samaritan. He shows compassion. He sees the need and acts promptly and more than appropriately. He binds the man's wounds, anoints the cuts with oil and wine, loads him on his own animal and takes him to an inn. He even stays the night with him and makes sure that the man will be treated until he recovers. "Which of these three, do you think, proved to be a neighbor to the man who fell among the robbers?" Jesus asked the lawyer, who responds contritely: "The one who showed him mercy." And Jesus said to him, "You go, and do likewise." (Lk 10:36–37). This is a powerful lesson about the ethics of Christian discipleship. We learn here about at least three central characteristics of the political disciple. *First*, she exhibits a strong link between knowing and doing; *secondly*, she expresses her love generously, and, *thirdly*, she does so in a way that does not distinguish between neighbor and non-neighbor.

The Active Ethics of Christian Discipleship

It is not enough to *know* the law which commands us to love God and neighbor. The Priest, the Levite (and the lawyer in the conversation) knew that full well. However, they were not prepared to put their knowledge into practice. Their orthodoxy did not lead, as it naturally should, to orthopraxy. Yet Jesus is very clear that those who are familiar with God's law ought to put it into practice. If you know these things," Jesus says elsewhere, "blessed are you if you *do* them" (Jn 13:17, emphasis added). Knowing leads organically to doing. Lived ethics is the central mark of a true disciple. *Secondly*, Jesus calls his disciples to a generous love. However, very much like the lawyer we intend to lower the bar for ethical involvement as we seek to limit the scope of our responsibilities as much as possible. Social psychologists have coined the term "diffusion of responsibility" to describe this phenomenon.[7] "There are plenty of other people in society who could play the good Samaritan, so why me?" But this just does not apply to Christian discipleship. Minimal obedience is just not good enough. Jesus demands exuberant love and compassion, akin to the love the good Samaritan showed and, in fact, to the sacrificial love Jesus himself has shown for us (1 Jn 3:16). "You go, and do likewise" is a challenging call to generous love, a love that does not hesitate to go over and beyond what is necessary. *Thirdly*, followers of Jesus love with a love that embraces both the close neighbor and the foreign neighbor. They exhibit a love that, in fact, does not know a non-neighbor.[8] Jesus' story calls us to be a neighbor to all, regardless of race, gender, color, nationality, religious conviction or non-conviction. The bottom line is this: If someone is in need, you

---

[7] John M. Darley and Bibb Latané, "Bystander intervention in emergencies: diffusion of responsibility," *Journal of Personality and Social Psychology* 8 (1968): 377–383.

[8] Pope Francis recently addressed this important point at his General Audience on Saint Peter's Square, where he discussed the passage in Luke 10:25–37 under the heading "Go and do likewise" (Wed, 27 April 2016); see https://w2.vatican.va/content/francesco/en/audiences/2016/documents/papa-francesco_20160427_udienza-generale.html, accessed 9 May 2016.

help that person. Full stop. We seem to find it difficult, though, to offer help to those who are less like us and more different from us. While we still might help those who are our very neighbors (family members, members of our own group, class, church, nation, or race), we are more reluctant to show compassion to those who are more distant neighbors. Here, we are blinded by racial biases and gender stereotypes; we exercise in-group-favoritism but outgroup derogation.[9] Consciously and even sub-consciously, as psychologists tell us, we exhibit xenophobic tendencies.[10] Still, God's Word again and again reminds us to love the neighbor who is foreign to us. We are to show compassion to the stranger in our midst. Why are we supposed to do that? Is there any evolutionary benefit in showing outgroup altruism? The straightforward answer to this question is that God loves the foreigner. "He defends the cause of the fatherless and the widow, and *loves the foreigner residing among you*" (Deut 10:18, emphasis added). God always sides with the oppressed, the less advantaged, the neglected and poor. God is a God of the underdog. In his own life Jesus always demonstrated God's love for the outcast. Jesus did not shrink back from touching the leper (Matt 8:3; Mk 1:41), or eating with sinners (Mk 2:15) or accepting the hospitality of a despised tax collector (Lk 19:1–10). Now if we love God (first command) we also love those whom God loves. If God loves the foreigner, so will we. There can be no such thing as a xenophobic Christian. Jesus' disciples are called to be xeno*philes*, they are commanded "to love those who are foreigners" (Deut 10:19a). They take to heart the commandment of old: "When a stranger sojourns with you in your land, you shall not do him wrong. You shall treat the stranger who sojourns with you as the native among you, and you shall love him as yourself, for you were strangers in the land of Egypt: I am the LORD your God." (Lev 19:33–34). From what has been said so far emerges the clear picture of how radical Christian discipleship is envisaged. Christian disciples are radical in their love and generosity towards all. And I

---

[9] Henri Tajfel and John C. Turner, "An integrative theory of intergroup conflict," in W. G. Austin and S. Worchel (Eds.), *The social psychology of intergroup relations* (Monterey, CA: Brooks/Cole, 1979), 33–47; Amélie Mummendey and Sabine Otten, "Aversive Discrimination," in M. B. Brewer and M. Hewstone (Eds.), *Emotion and Motivation* (Malden, MA: Blackwell, 2004), 298–318.

[10] Anthony G. Greenwald and Mahzarin R. Banaji, "Implicit Social Cognition: Attitudes, Self-Esteem, and Stereotypes," *Psychological Review* 102.1 (1995): 4–27; David M. Amodio and Patricia G. Devine, "Stereotyping and Evaluation in Implicit Race Bias: Evidence for Independent Constructs and Unique Effects on Behavior," *Journal of Personality and Social Psychology* 91.4 (2006): 652–661.

am convinced that the answer to the growing radicalization in Europe can only be a radical form of Christian discipleship.

Radical Discipleship

In fact, Jesus' call "Follow me!" is radical. It stands in opposition to the calls that go out from many a sugar-coated pulpit where we are promised that once we welcomed sweet Jesus into our hearts, financial freedom will follow suit. The opposite, in fact, might be the case. "If anyone comes to me and does not hate his own father and mother and wife and children and brothers and sisters, yes, and even his own life, he cannot be my disciple" (Lk 14:26). Following Jesus, Dietrich Bonhoeffer reminds us, involves not cheap grace but costly grace. "Cheap grace [*billige Gnade*] is the mortal enemy of our church. Our struggle today is for costly grace."[11] This is true even today. "But to you who are listening I say: Love your enemies, do good to those who hate you, bless those who curse you, pray for those who mistreat you." (Lk 6:27–28).[12] It does not get any more radical than this. This is a call to radical love and hospitality. Of course, if we were to take this radical call seriously and welcome so many foreigners with open arms, we might end up welcoming a Judas into our midst. We might run the risk of welcoming the traitor who does not share our view of a pluralist democratic society, of feminine emancipation and religious diversity. But can we ever fully eliminate this risk? Are we supposed to? Just because we are afraid that there might be two or three bad eggs among the migrants crossing our borders, does that mean we will not help the other 999,998 poor souls who have just escaped Assad's regime? Jesus never promised us perfect safety and protection from physical

---

[11] Bonhoeffer writes: "Cheap grace [*billige Gnade*] is the mortal enemy of our church. Our struggle today is for costly grace. Cheap grace means grace as bargain-basement goods, cut-rate forgiveness, cut-rate comfort, cut-rate sacrament; grace as the church's inexhaustible pantry, from which it is doled out by careless hands without hesitation or limit. It is grace without a price, without costs… Cheap grace means grace as doctrine, as principle, as system… It means God's love as merely a Christian idea of God. Those who affirm it have already had their sins forgiven… Cheap grace is, thus, denial of God's living word, denial of the incarnation of the word of God. Cheap grace means justification of sin but not of the sinner. Because grace alone does everything, everything can stay in its old ways. Cheap grace is the preaching of forgiveness without repentance; it is baptism without the discipline of the community; it is the Lord's Supper without confession of sin; it is absolution without personal confession. Cheap grace is grace without discipleship, grace without the cross, grace without the living, incarnate Jesus Christ." Dietrich Bonhoeffer, *Discipleship*, Vol. 4 of *Dietrich Bonhoeffer Works*, transl. from German edition, edited by Martin Kuske and Ilse Tödt, Engl. edition edited by Geffrey B. Kelly and John D. Godsey, transl. Barbara Green and Reinhard Krauss (Minneapolis, MN: Fortress, 2003), 43.

[12] "But I tell you, love your enemies and pray for those who persecute you" (Matt 5:44).

or psychological harm. On the contrary, those who follow in their master's footsteps, who was crucified, will suffer, too (Bonhoeffer knew that full well). The Apostle Peter makes this point very clear: "But if when you do good and suffer for it you endure, this is a gracious thing in the sight of God. For to this you have been called, because Christ also suffered for you, leaving you an example, so that you might follow in his steps" (1 Pet 2:20b-21). Suffering is always part of the deal. Having established the radical nature of Christian discipleship we are now in the position to add its significant political nature to the overall picture.

Political Discipleship

In recent decades, the subject of political theology and, in particular, political discipleship has enjoyed ever-growing attention. In his *Politics of Jesus* (1968), Mennonite theologian John Howard Yoder described the church as a political body.[13] Lutheran theologian Jürgen Moltmann offered in his lecture series on *Following Jesus Christ in the World Today* (1983) a critique of Luther's two kingdoms doctrine, putting forward his own view of a Christian messianic ethics.[14] In *The Desire for the Nations* (1996)[15], Anglican ethicist Oliver O'Donovan attempted to "re-state an Augustinian-Reformed approach to Church-state relations."[16] Graham Ward, Regius Professor of Divinity at Oxford, recently presented a manifesto for a *Politics of Discipleship* (2009) against the backdrop of increasing globalization and secularization.[17] Finally, last year, African-American theologian Vicent E. Bacote, who teaches at Wheaton College, published his little book, *The Political Disciple*,[18] in which he confesses that Abraham Kuyper's theology had left a deep impression on his view of church and politics.[19] In fact, Bacote

---

[13] John H. Yoder, *The Politics of Jesus* (Grand Rapids, MI: Eerdmans, 1972).

[14] Jürgen Moltmann, *The Politics of Discipleship and Discipleship in Politics: Jürgen Moltmann Lectures in Dialogue with Mennonite Scholars*, ed. Willard M. Swartley (Eugene, OR: Wipf and Stock, 2006), 3–18.

[15] Oliver O'Donovan, *The Desire of the Nations: Rediscovering the Roots of Political Theology* (Cambridge: Cambridge University Press, 1996).

[16] Luke Bretherton, "Introduction: Oliver O'Donovan's Political Theology and the Liberal Imperative," *Political Theology* 9.3 (October 2008): 268.

[17] Ward, *The Politics of Discipleship*.

[18] Bacote, *The Political Disciple: A Theology of Public Life* (Grand Rapids, MI: Zondervan, 2015).

[19] Bacote, *The Political Disciple: A Theology of Public Life*, 22–29.

writes that Kuyper's word were "like oxygen" to him.[20] Bacote stands, *pars pro toto*, for a new generation of pastors and theologians who rediscover Kuyper's heritage at the outset of a new millennium. Kuyper's emphasis on common grace and on sphere sovereignty, his view of a "culture-affirming Christianity,"[21] that combines spiritual vigor with social engagement speaks powerfully into the challenges of our present age. For this reason I consider it very promising to take a closer look at political discipleship through the Kuyperian lens.

Abraham Kuyper

Abraham Kuyper was convinced that we all share a particular responsibility towards the broader *polis*, that we all have a special role to play on the public sphere, and he clearly acted upon it (he clearly saw the link between knowing and doing we mentioned earlier). Originally ordained as a Reformed minister, Kuyper's broad interests led him to found a newspaper, a political party, and a university, while he also served for some years as Prime Minster of the Netherlands (between 1902 and 1905). His biography tells the story of a political disciple who saw no conflict between a passionate engagement in the church *and* for the state. Throughout his life, Kuyper was keen to counter any dualistic views that distinguished too sharply between the kingdom of the world and the kingdom of Christ, which only left behind confused disciples who were unsure of their calling. "Every division must be opposed with every possible power," Kuyper argues, "[t]emporal and eternal life, our life in the world and in the church, religious and civic life, Church and State and so much more, *may not be separated.*"[22] Kuyper's holistic view of gospel proclamation *and* social responsibility is both liberating and challenging. "It is one and the same *I* who is a citizen of the country and a member of the church," he claims.[23] "The Calvinist cannot shut himself up in his church and abandon the world to its fate," Kuyper states. "He feels, rather, in his high calling to push the development of this world to an even

---

[20] Bacote, *The Political Disciple: A Theology of Public Life*, 24.

[21] Bacote, *The Political Disciple: A Theology of Public Life*, 20.

[22] Abraham Kuyper, *De gemeene gratie*, part ii, 638, quoted in Gerard Dekker and George Harinck, "The Position of the Church as Institute in Society: A Comparison between Bonhoeffer and Kuyper," *The Princeton Seminary Bulletin* 28.1 (2007): 90.

[23] Abraham Kuyper, *Abraham Kuyper: A Centennial Reader*, ed. James D. Bratt (Grand Rapids, MI: Eerdmans, 1998), 185.

higher stage, and to do this in constant accordance with God's ordinance, for the sake of God, upholding, in the midst of so much painful corruption, everything that is honorable, lovely, and of good report among men."[24] Kuyper's message was originally directed at Christian escapists who were busy day-dreaming of their heavenly citizenship while forgetting their earthly calling. And I think this message is just as valid today as it was back then.[25] Kuyper warns us against a "monastic flight *from* the world" and encourages us to serve "God *in* the world, in every position in life."[26] This is what makes a disciple a political disciple. We are now concerned about the proclamation of the gospel *and* social justice, about spiritual growth *and* the welfare of the migrants, about liturgy *and* a fair distribution of wealth. Political disciples are "duty-bound to honor an operation of divine grace in human civic life by which the curse of sin, and sin itself, is restrained even though the link with salvation is lacking."[27] The crucial—and obvious—question is, of course: How are we going to achieve a balance here? How can we engage in the public square without becoming Social Gospellers?

Organic Political Disciples

I find Kuyper's distinction between the church as institute and organism helpful in this context.[28] Kuyper claims that the church has an institutional and an organic mode of existence.[29] The church

---

[24] Abraham Kuyper, *Lectures on Calvinism* (Grand Rapids, MI: Eerdmans, 1931), 73.

[25] Oliver O'Donovan recently lamented that "[t]he neo-orthodoxy that put Christ as the center without putting him at the center of the created world gave birth to an ethics that danced like an angel on the head of a needle, wholly lacking worldly dimensions and focused solely on a conversion-encounter with the cross." O'Donovan, *Self, World, and Time: Ethics as Theology*, Vol.1 (Grand Rapids: Eerdmans, 2013), 93.

[26] Kuyper, *Lectures on Calvinism*, 30 (emphasis original).

[27] Kuyper, *Abraham Kuyper: A Centennial Reader*, 193.

[28] I have discussed this important Kuyperian distinction in more detail elsewhere. See my essay, "The Christian as *homo politicus*: Abraham Kuyper and Democratic Imbalance in Post-Democratic Times," in *The Kuyper Center Review*, volume 4: Calvinism and Democracy, edited by John Bowlin (Grand Rapids, MI: Eerdmans, 2014), 67–85.

[29] "[T]he Ecclesia visibilis has a twofold form of existence, firstly as organism and secondly as institute. As organism, where you can observe its organic workings in the people and in the relationships among them, and as institute, in as far as it has, through independent organization, developed into a specific form." Abraham Kuyper, *Encyclopedie der Heilige Godgeleerdheid*, part III (Kampen: Kok, 1908/09), 204; quoted in Gerard Dekker and George Harinck, "The Position of the Church as Institute in Society: A Comparison between Bonhoeffer and Kuyper," 91. See also Kuyper, *Abraham Kuyper: A Centennial Reader*, 193–194; James D. Bratt, *Abraham Kuyper, Modern Calvinist, Christian Democrat* (Grand Rapids, MI: Eerdmans, 2013), 56–59.

as institute focuses on its main mission, namely the preaching of the Word of God and the administration of the sacraments.[30] As such, the church is holy, separated from the world and set apart for God. The church as organism, however, permeates the world as it is made up of disciples who are active in society: they participate in political grassroots movements and town hall meetings, they voice their concerns as journalists and bloggers. "Whereas the Church as institute is removed from the world and therefore stands opposite to it," Kuyper writes, "the Church as organism enters into the life of the world in exactly the opposite way, turns it around, gives it another form, raises it and sanctifies it."[31] This distinction is helpful insofar as it enables the church to do what it does best and what it is called to do, while it also sets political disciples free to go out and transform society. They go out and contribute to the flourishing of human communities as the "organic church," or, as Graham Ward put it, the "apophatic body of Christ in action."[32] This is, in fact, a language that Kuyper would have approved of. Kuyper's theology of active political discipleship is rooted in a clear understanding of the church as Christ's body in action. "The Church," writes Kuyper, "is thus not just a gathering of Jesus' followers; no, it has become in the full sense of the term the body of Christ, the rich organism wherein not just his spirit but Christ himself lives on."[33] For this reason, "[n]o area of life," Kuyper contends, "remains alien to the Christian!"[34] Since Christ is active in this world, his body is an active church, a "sanctified Church"[35] that enters "every terrain of life."[36] Political disciples have not only realized that God is still graciously inclined towards this fallen world, but, much more importantly, that they are members of Christ's body and as such God's instrument to extend his loving hand towards creation.

---

[30] See Dekker and Harinck, "The Position of the Church as Institute in Society," 93.

[31] Abraham Kuyper, *De gemeene gratie*, part III, 424–425; quoted in Dekker and Harinck, "The Position of the Church as Institute in Society," 96.

[32] Ward, *The Politics of Discipleship*, 258.

[33] Kuyper quoted in Bratt, *Abraham Kuyper, Modern Calvinist, Christian Democrat*, 174.

[34] Kuyper quoted in Bratt, *Abraham Kuyper, Modern Calvinist, Christian Democrat*, 58.

[35] Kuyper quoted in Bratt, *Abraham Kuyper, Modern Calvinist, Christian Democrat*, 54.

[36] Kuyper quoted in Bratt, *Abraham Kuyper, Modern Calvinist, Christian Democrat*, 59.

Conclusion

Europe in 2016 is under pressure. There are still thousands of refugees seeking shelter, the European Union member states are still strident and their societies are growing ever more unsettled, which plays into the hands of right-wing parties who are recently gaining considerable support.[37] I have argued that Christian disciples are called to play a major role when it comes to tackling this crisis, and I have put forward an understanding of discipleship that is radical, political, and organic. In my view, it is crucial that we emphasize the radical nature of the Christian call to discipleship again. Followers of Christ live in what Dietrich Bonhoeffer has called the "this-worldliness" (*Diesseitigkeit*) of human existence.[38] They follow Christ to the difficult places and practice *kenosis* for the good of their close and distant neighbor. The dramatic situation of the migrants calls for acts of radical hospitality that have an eschatological bearing. "'Lord, when did we see you hungry and feed you, or thirsty and give you drink? And when did we see you a stranger and welcome you, or naked and clothe you?" (Matt 25:37–38). "[T]he church's goal is to be God's peace in the broken places," writes Mark Gornik, "and to bear witness to the kingdom of God. It sides not with the privileged and powerful but with those the world counts as nothing. This is the politics of Christ and the cross."[39] Christian disciples are political disciples. They do not hide in their churches but emerge as concerned citizens, giving a voice to those who are speechless in face of persecution and oppression. Richard J. Mouw is right when he argues that Christians must actively "work together as agents of this restorative program that encompasses the whole range of cultural involvement."[40] And here is certainly room (and necessity!) for creativity. Political disciples politely but firmly oppose the claims of right-wing movements such as those of PEGIDA, AfD, Marine le Pen and their allies. They articulate powerfully but respectfully the Christian point of view on the public

---

[37] See http://www.bbc.com/news/world-europe-36150807 and http://www.theguardian.com/news/datablog/2016/jan/26/rightwing-parties-are-on-the-rise-but-they-wont-win-power-without-women, both accessed 9 May 2016.

[38] Dietrich Bonhoeffer to Eberhard Bethge, 21 July 1944, in Bonhoeffer, *Letters and Papers from Prison*, The Enlarged Edition, ed. Eberhard Bethge (London: SCM, 1971), 370.

[39] Mark R. Gornik, *To live in peace: Biblical Faith and the Changing Inner City* (Grand Rapids, MI: Eerdmans, 2002), 124.

[40] Richard J. Mouw, *The Challenges of Cultural Discipleship: Essays in the Line of Abraham Kuyper* (Grand Rapids, MI: Eerdmans, 2012), 20.

stage, via Instagram, Facebook and Twitter, using all the means available. They pursue "generous justice" (Tim Keller) as they actively participate in local civic life, in round tables, town hall meetings, pressure groups and neighborhood groups. They happily volunteer in refugee centers and enjoy helping Syrian children with their homework. In short, they are witnesses to Jesus Christ through "a network of ever different relations of agape" (Charles Taylor).[41] I have, finally, argued for an organic understanding of Christian political discipleship. Organic in the sense that political disciples are organically united with Christ; they are members of his body, and as such, the *missio dei* becomes their mission;[42] they love those whom Christ loves, they care for those for whom Christ cares. As members of the organic church, Christian disciples "seek the welfare of the city" (Jer 29:7) and pray for a positive transformation of human societies.[43] This world yearns for radical Christian political disciples who welcome strangers in the name of Christ. And the disciples, in turn, eagerly look forward to the day when they hear their King saying to them: "Truly, I say to you, as you did it to one of the least of these my brothers, you did it to me." (Matt 25:40)

---

[41] Ward, *The Politics of Discipleship*, 259.

[42] Nicholas Wolterstorff reminds us: "We are workers in God's cause, his peace-workers. The *missio Dei* is our mission." Wolterstorff, *Until Justice and Peace Embrace: The Kuyper Lectures for 1981 Delivered at the Free University of Amsterdam* (Grand Rapids, MI: Eerdmans, 1983), 72.

[43] Graham Ward emphasizes the importance of prayer as crucial instrument when it comes to the transformation of our culture. He describes prayer as "the *Urgrund* of Christian discipleship: we live and act as transistors for the transformation of the world through Christ." Ward, *Politics of Discipleship*, 281–282.

BOOK REVIEWS

Chenoweth, Ben. *The Ephesus Scroll* (Melbourne: MST Press), 2016 (repr.) and *The Corinth Letters* (Melbourne: MST Press), 2015.

The Ephesus Scroll is an historical novel that forges two horizons. The first is set in the late first-century AD, when a courier is entrusted with a scroll containing the Book of Revelation to be read in the seven churches of Asia Minor. These churches were facing bitter persecution from the Roman empire. The novel shows how the text of Revelation, with its ominous warnings and great encouragements, related directly to the experiences of these early Christian communities.

The second is set in the early twenty-first century AD when a young Russian couple come across a stone box discovered some time ago in Ephesus, and which contains an early copy of the Book of Revelation. It portrays the efforts of these twenty-first century believers to make sense of Revelation in their own day. As the book moves between the two horizons, it provides an explanation of the contents of the book of Revelation that is rooted in the historical context and reflects sound New Testament scholarship.

The Corinth Letters is also an historical novel that forges two horizons, that of tensions existing in the Corinthian church of the mid first-century on the one hand, and the work of young people assisting with an archaeological dig at ancient Corinth in the early twenty-first century on the other. It provides a very readable account of the historical background to Paul's letters to the Corinthians and the complex relationship that existed between the Corinthian church and its founding apostle. It also reflects sound New Testament scholarship, and will be helpful to all seeking to understand Paul's letters.

Both these books can be read simply for the enjoyment of well-written historian novels, as well as for an appreciation of the historical background to these New Testament books. People will find both hard to put down, not something that can be said about most New Testament textbooks. Both books remind me, in some ways, of Gerd Theissen's book, *The Shadow of the Galilean*, which is likewise an historical novel, informed by New Testament scholarship, providing helpful and readable background material for the study of the Gospels. I warmly commend Ben Chenoweth's books to all interested readers of the New Testament.

Colin Kruse
Melbourne School of Theology

Crysdale, Cynthia S. W., and Neil Ormerod. *Creator God, Evolving World* (Minneapolis: Fortress Press, 2013).

I didn't really know what to expect from this book, which I picked off a bookshelf on spec about a year ago both out of interest and because it was on the discount shelf, and I love a bargain. So often the good stuff, that people ought to read but don't, is found there. And I noticed that one of the authors, Neil Ormerod, is an Aussie, and teaches at the Australian Catholic University in Sydney, while Crysdale is based at the University of the South in Sewanee, Tennessee, USA. The perspective of the book is Catholic, with an appreciation for the deep tradition of Christian thought back through influential figures such as Thomas Aquinas, as well as what looks to me, as one not scientifically trained, like a solid feel for the sciences (e.g. biology, physics) and the philosophy of science.

As the title suggests, biological evolution is taken for granted in this book, and for some evangelical readers that may be a deal-breaker. I personally see Neo-Darwinism as another knowledge paradigm, like so many composed by humans over the years to make sense of their world. One day it will give way to a replacement paradigm, though many of its composing elements will be carried over into whatever follows. So a further century or two of history will give its verdict on which parts of the Neo-Darwinian synthesis deserve to be retained and which ones are no longer persuasive. So this was not something that stopped me reading.

What I liked about the book was the depth of thinking it displayed in the philosophy of science, or you might say, theology of science. The authors are influenced by twentieth-century Catholic thinker Bernard Lonergan, and after reading the book, I feel more inclined to explore Lonergan's thought, too. Another clear influence to go with Lonergan in modern times and Aquinas in medieval ones is

Augustine, and the authors' most interesting contribution builds on Augustine's thought.

If you have ever read Augustine's *Confessions*, an essential item on anyone's bucket list, you might remember Augustine's meditations on the relationship of God to time. The critics of the day were lambasting Christian belief in creation by asking what God had been occupied with for all those aeons of eternity past prior to the apparently impromptu decision to create a world, as if to alleviate His boredom. Augustine makes the very wise philosophical reply that we ought to think of time as part of creation. If God creates time with the world and as part of the world, the question of what God was doing before creation with all that spare previous eternity becomes null. There was no 'before' as such.[1]

This entails believing that God transcends time as readily as He transcends universal space. Just as He cannot be found in a certain location in our physical universe, He is not embedded in any of our 'nows'; He is above time. I think this is the right way to think, and solves some theological dilemmas, but let me tell you why Crysdale and Ormerod hold to this.

They are concerned about the trend in science and religion circles to treat God as if He is travelling through time as humans do, immersed in a 'present', looking back at a 'past', anticipating and planning for a 'future'. And rather than knowing the future infallibly, God has to adapt to it as it comes. The future in this scheme is fundamentally unknowable, since it isn't out there somewhere, pre-programmed. The present comes into being, as it were, right out of the blue. So even God can't know precisely what's about to happen. It is by definition unknowable.

In what I think is a brilliant, though somewhat obvious move, our authors point out that in the context of relativity theory, there is no single, fixed 'present' that is a universal reference point for all observers. Time may dilate dependent on the influence of gravity or differential rates of travel in comparison with the speed of light. It can in fact tick over faster for one observer than another. So whose 'now' is to be the authoritative 'now' that is occupied by God? No, it is a mistake to pin God to a certain point of time. God is outside of the flow in which we are immersed and in which we must, as it were, ride downstream to where the current is taking us.

---

[1] *Confessions* 11.13.15–14.17; *City of God* 11.6.

Here's the surprising place to which this leads. I sometimes wonder about the seeming distance and/or silence of God. The two seem closely related. But the authors point out that ironically, it is in admitting that God is *not* embedded in our time and space that makes it possible to understand how God can be near to us. If God were somewhere in space, it would require a spacecraft odyssey to go and find God, or we would be limited to awaiting His next visit from some impossible distance, if we wished to experience His presence. (If this is wrong, and theologically I think it is, we must think carefully how we are going to put words to the continued 'embodiedness' of the risen Christ!) If God were somewhere in time, we might well feel that that time was 2,000 years ago when Christ walked the earth, and that the subsequent millennia have been marked more by His absence, and a lot of churchy business, than by His presence.

But if God transcends time, then every moment of history is equally real and equally present to God. The moment of our birth, and the moment of our death. The birth of civilization on some Mesopotamian waterway, and the birth of the first Mars colony. And, for that matter, the birth of Jesus, his crucifixion, death, and resurrection. Every moment equally and eternally present to God, and God in turn able to be equally present in our every personal moment.

> While God's response *to us* is itself eternal and unchanging, it unfolds *for us* in the fullness of time.[2]

My appreciation to the authors for reminding me of this. They say a lot of other things besides, and the reader might wish for a more robust doctrine of sin, or a fuller Christology to go with their thinking about the being of God. But this book crept up on me and made me think, and unlike most books I read, left me encouraged in spirit.

Andrew Brown
Melbourne School of Theology

---

[2] Cynthia S. W. Crysdale and Neil Ormerod. *Creator God, Evolving World* (Minneapolis: Fortress Press, 2013), 128.

Mason, Karen. *Preventing Suicide: A Handbook for Pastors, Chaplains and Pastoral Counselors* (Downers Grove, IL: Inter Varsity Press), 2014.

As a committed educator in the Christian community on suicide prevention, intervention, and postvention care of those bereaved by suicide, to equip caregivers to minister into this challenging area, Mason's book is considered a worthy addition to any minister's library.

Mason, a psychologist, and associate professor of counseling and psychology at Gordon-Conwell Theological Seminary having worked in the mental health field for twenty-six years brings her expertise to this complex discussion to show practically how pastoral caregivers can be agents of hope to people at-risk to suicide. The book first addresses foundational issues in discussions and approaches to suicide before progressing to the more practical component where Mason then shares numerous anecdotes from not only her experience with suicidal people but also those of Christian caregivers in a variety of ministry settings.

The first four chapters are vital for caregivers to explore before engaging practically. Chapter one addresses commonly held preconceived ideas as to who dies by suicide. Here Mason explores what role race, gender, and factors such as biology and mental health play in predicting whether someone will die by suicide. Chapter two shatters ten suicide myths with a primary focus on people within the Christian community evidencing suicidal-ideations (*someone who thinks about suicide, has a plan and the means to carry it out*), which can tragically end in death. These myths are debunked in the "light of Bible and science." Chapter three flows on from the examination of myths about Christians experiencing suicidal-ideations to a theological discussion about Christians who sadly take their life and the historical responses from the church as to their future hope. These three chapters are critical for caregivers to explore, as preconceived ideas and a minister's operating theology can be a hindrance to offering people with suicidal-ideations help, and their readiness to extend comfort to those bereaved by suicide. Self-examination precedes practical engagement. Chapter four then offers an understanding of the historical and contemporary theories to suicide and the importance of a bio-psycho-social-spiritual approach in caring for at-risk people in the Christian community.

Chapters five through to nine immerse the reader in anecdotes and a multitude of valuable practical strategies in caring for the following five people groups: someone in a suicide crisis (chapter 5); a survivor of a suicide attempt (chapter 6); a caregiver (chapter 7); those bereaved by suicide (chapter 8); and the faith community (chapter 9). While some strategies overlap, each group have needs specific to them, which merit understanding when engaging care.

Mason writes in language easily understood by any caregiver with or without prior knowledge on this topic. People with prior understanding or working in this field will no doubt find amongst the strategies offered something that will contribute to their existing repertoire of approaches. Each chapter is equipped with discussion questions that can be used either in a group setting or for personal reflection. Additional resources are also offered for the reader to refer to if needed. Whilst noting many websites as avenues for referring people in crisis, this will not benefit those located outside of the United States. Caregivers will need to identify appropriate resources from within their community or from country specific websites committed to suicide prevention.

With an increasing number of people struggling with suicidal-ideations, tragically even within the Christian community, it is needful for caregivers to equip themselves with the relevant tools to be able to intervene when they find themselves confronted with someone in crisis. This book is certainly a step in that direction.

Astrid Staley
Harvest Bible College

Rau, Gerald. *Mapping the Origins Debate* (Leicester: InterVarsity, 2012).

I dare anyone to read all the books available on creation, evolution, the book of Genesis, or science and religion. There would hardly be time if you did nothing else. So it isn't uncommon to get that "I've heard all this before" feeling.

However, this approachable book by Gerald Rau, past adjunct professor teaching biology at Wheaton College in the US, with a doctorate from Cornell University, stood out for its clarity on the topic of origins. I suppose it should; his current role is "founder and chief editor at Professional English International, Inc., a team providing high quality editing services in English academic writing, based at National Chung Cheng University in Chiayi, Taiwan."[3]

Rau lays out the state of play in creation-evolution discussions using six categories that prove quite helpful:

1. *Naturalistic evolution*, or atheistic evolution, the Richard Dawkins style of evolution that just happens to have happened, with no-one intending it. Our world is an accidental freak of nature, and here we are scratching our heads wondering what happened.

2. *Non-teleological evolution*, which is a kind of deistic version amenable to process theologians. God is responsible for creation, but more or less just lit the fuse that set off the Big Bang. He didn't set the course for where it would end up, other than, says Rau at one point, that he wanted sentient life to appear.

3. *Planned evolution* holds that God has set up the universe from the start to lead to the outcomes he sought, including the appearance of humans. So this is a teleological version, one with an intended outcome, but the system is so well designed that God need not, and does not, intervene subsequently.

4. *Directed evolution* is interventionist as well as teleological, permitting that God actively directs the evolutionary process.

5. *Old-earth creationism* effectively breaks the links, or better, finds significant missing links, in the evolutionary chain. The earth is indeed old on this scheme, but major new stages such as the Cambrian explosion, and in particular, the first humans, reflect the direct creative work of God. There is no true evolutionary tree.

6. Finally, *young-earth creationism* holds to a literal Genesis creation week and would connect the various Old Testament genealogies to come up with quite a short world

---

[3] https://www.ivpress.com/cgi-ivpress/author.pl/author_id=6583.

chronology. We might say that earth history is not any older than human history in any real sense here.

Rau proves this schema to be quite workable as he explains what the general evidence is, and then what each model has to say, about four areas of inquiry:

- The origin of the universe
- The origin of life
- The origin of species
- The origin of humans.

Rau says that he is pitching this book at late high schoolers and college students, so I was a little worried that it might come across as simplistic. But my sense is that Rau is quite competent to speak on a range of areas; I learned a lot about such things as recent developments in comparisons between the recently-sequenced genomes of chimpanzees and humans. To put the outcome of that point very briefly, the two sets of code (3 billion base pairs in the human genome v. 2.7 billion base pairs for the chimp) have quite a range of variations from one another, yet are still alike enough that it makes sense to speak of which sequences are the same and where the differences lie. Rau offers many intriguing and often readily accessible references for follow-up on such points.

Let me close with one group out of many apt quotes I might have chosen, suitable because it reflects my own thinking so well:

> The question of origins is a puzzle, and it is clear that no model has put the whole puzzle together yet... We are all working on the same puzzle and must eventually work together if it is to be completed... There would not be a debate unless there were reasonable arguments on each side.[4]

I often find myself wanting to concede to each end of the spectrum, strict creation and the evolutionary paradigm, that I am convinced on some points and not at all persuaded by others. I see various pieces that look as though they belong in the puzzle, but I haven't seen anyone properly solve the puzzle yet. That's a hard sell for others, because our hearers are sometimes expecting that, while they haven't themselves figured out the puzzle of origins yet, there must be an expert who has, and maybe it's us. As a theological educator, I have certainly learned a few things about the issue, but I

---

[4] Gerald Rau, *Mapping the Origins Debate* (Leicester: InterVarsity, 2012), 153–155.

don't have that ready-to-order solution that is often sought. Perhaps a little healthy humility is in order here – to let God be God, the One who knows the answers, and not presume to know too much. Rau complains late in the book that it's chiefly hubris (i.e. pride) that fuels the fights that thrive in this area, and I wonder if he might be right.

What Rau made me feel that perhaps this cautious, piecemeal approach to the discovery of the truth about origins has some legitimacy.

Andrew Brown
Melbourne School of Theology

INVITATION FOR PAPERS

MST's journal *PARADOSIS* brings together theological minds in the on-going advancement in Christian thought and practice. We believe that theological and biblical disciplines should never exist on their own; they require a broader field of vision. Therefore *PARADOSIS* will showcase articles in biblical studies and theology which manifest this.

Particular interest will be shown in those submissions which are of an inter-disciplinary nature, especially those that connect biblical, historical or theological insights with current church trends or challenges to Christian thought in a wide variety of current contexts.

The majority of papers in each edition will coalesce around certain themes and the Executive Editor will receive suggestions regarding potential future themes or guest authors for individual issues. Each issue will have its own Issue Editor on her/his own field of expertise (proposed themes for the coming years are listed below). In this way the journal will examine reasonable expressions of the proposed theme from the range of theological disciplines, framework and perspective to suit a scholarly, **student** or pastoral readership.

Articles accepted for publication are 'peer reviewed', being read and assessed by at least one pertinent scholar in the appropriate field.

We extend our invitation to all, both in Australia and internationally.

Dr Justin Tan
Executive Editor

2017/8: *Christian/Biblical Ethics*
2019: *Christian Spirituality*

NOTES FOR CONTRIBUTORS

Submission requirements

Manuscript

> Papers should not exceed 8000 words, although the Editor retains the discretion to publish papers that vary from this length.

> It is preferable that submissions be prepared in Microsoft Word format. When using citation management software tools, please remove all field codes before submission.

All papers are to be written in English, and must conform to MST style requirements. This can be found on the MST website (http://www.mst.edu.au/wp-content/uploads/2015/07/MST-Essay-Guide-15.pdf). Refer also to the style used in the current issue.

> Any Greek and Hebrew words written in original script should use SBL Greek/Hebrew (or SBL BibLit) Unicode font. An English translation should be provided in brackets where the meaning is not readily apparent from the context. No transliteration is necessary unless judged necessary.

> Authors are advised to use gender inclusive and non-discriminatory language.

> Any visuals should be integrated into the document, or sent separately as separate jpg or gif files with an explanation as to their position in the paper.

Submission

> Papers to be considered for inclusion are to be submitted directly to the Executive Editor (jtan@mst.edu.au), via electronic mail.

> A declaration that the submitted articles are your own work and that you have acknowledged the work/s of others used in the articles in the references, etc. must be included with any submission.

> A covering letter that includes the author's full name, titles, affiliations, with complete mailing addresses, including email, telephone and facsimile numbers, should be attached to the paper.

Review of Submissions

    All submissions will be sent to referees for anonymous recommendation.

    The Editor holds the right to make editorial corrections to accepted submissions.

Copyright

PARADOSIS is published by MST Press, the publishing arm of the Melbourne School of Theology. The copyright for any published papers will remain with the author. MST publishes these papers on the following conditions:

- They do not appear elsewhere (including web pages) for 12 months from the date of publication in *PARADOSIS*.
- Whenever they are printed elsewhere (including web pages), the following notice will be included: "This article first appeared in the __ issue of the *PARADOSIS* series".
- MST retains the right to use the paper in any MST publications, reprints, or in electronic form (ie. Online, CD-Rom, etc.).
- MST retains the right to use a portion or description of the paper with the author's name in our promotional material.
- Authors are themselves responsible for obtaining permission to reproduce copyright material from other sources.
- The author will be presented with one copy of the publication.

Disclaimer

The opinions and conclusions published in the *PARADOSIS* series are those of the authors and do not necessarily represent the views of the Editors or the Melbourne School of Theology.